Henry Marshall Ward

The Oak

A Popular Introduction to Forest-Botany

Henry Marshall Ward

The Oak
A Popular Introduction to Forest-Botany

ISBN/EAN: 9783744674102

Printed in Europe, USA, Canada, Australia, Japan

Cover: Foto ©Andreas Hilbeck / pixelio.de

More available books at **www.hansebooks.com**

THE OAK

A POPULAR INTRODUCTION TO FOREST-BOTANY

BY

H. MARSHALL WARD, M.A. F.R.S. F.L.S.

LATE FELLOW OF CHRIST'S COLLEGE, CAMBRIDGE
PROFESSOR OF BOTANY AT THE ROYAL INDIAN ENGINEERING COLLEGE, COOPER'S HILL.

LONDON
KEGAN PAUL, TRENCH, TRÜBNER, & CO. Ltd.
PATERNOSTER HOUSE, CHARING CROSS ROAD
1892

CONTENTS

THE OAK

CHAPTER I

INTRODUCTION

FAMOUS in poetry and prose alike, the oak must always be for Englishmen a subject of interest, around which historical associations of the most varied character are grouped; but although what may be termed the sentimental aspect of the 'British oak' is not likely to disappear even in these days of ironclads and veneering, it must be allowed that the popular admiration for the sturdy tree is to-day a very different feeling from the veneration with which it was regarded in ancient times; and that, with the calmer and more thoughtful ways of looking at this and other objects of superstition, a certain air of romance seems to have disappeared which to so many would still present a tempting charm. It is not to these latter alone that our few existing ancient oaks are so attractive, however, and a slight acquaintance with the oaken roofs and carvings of some of our historical edifices affords ample proof that the indefinable charm exercised on us by what has proved so lasting, is a real one and deep-seated in the Saxon nature. In fact, everything about the oak is suggestive of durability and sturdy hardiness, and, like so many objects of human worship in the earlier days of man's emergence from a savage state, the oak instinctively attracts us. The attraction is no doubt complex, taking its origin in the value of its acorns and timber to our early forefathers, not unaffected by the artistic beauty of the foliage and habit of the tree, and the forest life of our ancestors, to say nothing of the more modern sentiment aroused when ships of war were built almost entirely of heart of oak; for the Aryan race seems to have used and valued both the fruit and the wood from very early times, and both Celt and Saxon preserved the traditional regard for them. Memories of our Anglo-Saxon ancestors are still found in the English and German names for the tree and its fruit, as seen by comparing the Anglo-Saxon *āc* or *œc*, the name of the oak, with the English word, and with the German *Eiche* on the one hand, and with acorn (*Eichel*) on the other. In early days, moreover, there were vast oak forests in our island and on the Continent, and, although these have been almost cleared away so far as England is concerned, there are still ancient oaks in this country, some of which must date from Saxon times or thereabouts, and the oak is still one of the commonest trees in France, parts of Germany, and some other districts in Europe.

This is not the place to go further into what may be called the folk-lore of the oak—a subject which would supply material for a large volume—but it may be remarked that giant or veteran oaks are still to be found (or were until quite recently) in Gloucestershire, Yorkshire, and on Dartmoor and other places, and a very fair idea of what an old oak forest must have been like may be gathered from a visit to the New Forest in Hampshire, or even to some parts of Windsor Forest.

As so often happens in the study of science, we have in the oak a subject for investigation which presents features of intense interest at every turn, and however much the new mode of looking at the tree may at first sight appear to be opposed to the older one, it will be found that the story of the oak as an object of biological study is at least not less fascinating than its folk-lore. With this idea in view, I propose to set before the reader in the following chapters a short account of what is most worth attention in the anatomy and physiology of the oak, as a forest tree which has been so thoroughly investigated that we may confidently accept it as a type.

In carrying out this idea there are several possible modes of procedure, but perhaps the following will recommend itself as that best adapted to the requirements of a popular book, and as a natural way of tracing the various events in the life-history of a plant so complex as is the tree.

First, the acorn will be described as an object with

a certain structure and composition, and capable of
behaving in a definite manner when placed in the
ground, and under certain circumstances, in virtue of its
physiological properties and of the action of the environment upon its structure. The germinated acorn
gives rise to the seedling or young oak, and we shall
proceed to regard this, again, as a subject for botanical
study. It consists of certain definite parts or organs,
each with its peculiar structure, tissues, &c., and each
capable of behaving in a given manner under proper
conditions. The study of the seedling leads naturally
to that of the sapling and the tree, and the at first
comparatively simple root-system, stem, and leaves, now
become complex and large, and each demands careful
attention in order that we may trace the steps by which
the tree is evolved from the plantlet. A section will therefore be devoted to the root-system of the tree, its disposi-
tion, structure, functions, and accessories; another section will be occupied in describing the trunk, branches,
buds, and leaves, and their co-relations and functions;
the inflorescence and flowers will demand the space of
another chapter, and then it will be necessary to treat
of various matters of importance in separate chapters as
follows:—The timber must be considered with respect to
its composition, structure, uses, and functions; then
the cortex and bark have to be described and their
origin and development explained. These subjects
naturally lead to that of the growth in thickness of the
tree—a matter of some complexity, and not to be under-

stood without the foregoing knowledge of structure.
Following what has been said concerning the normal
structure and life-processes of the tree, we may turn to
the investigation of its cultivation and the diseases
which attack it, concluding with a necessarily brief
chapter on the systematic position of the British oak
and its immediate allies, and some remarks on its geographical distribution at the present time.

Of course, many points which will turn up in the
course of the exposition will have to be shortly dealt
with, as the object of the book is to touch things with
a light hand ; but it is hoped that, this notwithstanding,
the reader may obtain a useful glimpse into the domain
of modern botanical science and the problems with which
forest botany is concerned, and with which every properly
trained forester ought to be thoroughly acquainted.

The oak, as is well known, is a slow-growing, dicotyledonous tree of peculiar spreading habit, and very
intolerant of shade (Plate I.). It may reach a great age
—certainly a thousand years—and still remain sound
and capable of putting forth leafy shoots.

The root-system consists normally of a deep principal
or tap root and spreading lateral roots, which become
very thick and woody and retain a remarkably strong
hold on the soil when the latter is a suitable deep,
tenacious loam with rocks in it. They are intolerant of
anything like stagnant water, however, and will succeed
better in sandy loam and more open soils than in richer
ones improperly drained.

The shoot-system consists of the stem and all that it
supports.   The stem or trunk is usually irregular when
young, but becomes more symmetrical later, and after
fifty years or so it normally consists of a nearly straight
and cylindrical shaft with a broad base and spreading
branches.   The main branches come out at a wide angle,
and spread irregularly, with a zigzag course, due to the
short annual growths of the terminal shoots and the
few axillary buds behind, and also to the fact that many
of the axillary lateral buds develop more slowly than
their parent shoot, and are cut off in the autumn.
Another phenomenon which co-operates in producing
the very irregular spreading habit of the branches is the
almost total suppression of some of the closely-crowded
buds; these may remain dormant for many years, and
then, under changed circumstances, put forth accessory
shoots.   Such shoots are very commonly seen on the
stems and main branches of large oaks to which an
increased accession of light is given by the thinning out
of surrounding trees.

The short ovoid buds develop into shoots so short
that they are commonly referred to as tufts of leaves,
though longer summer shoots often arise later.   The
latter are also called Lammas shoots.   The crown of
foliage is thus very dense, and the bright green of the
leaves in early summer is very characteristic, especially
in connection with the horizontal, zigzag spreading
of the shoots.

While still young the tree is apt to keep its dead

leaves on the branches through the winter, or at least until a severe frost followed by a thaw brings them down. The buds, leaves, and flowers are all much attacked by gall-forming insects, many different kinds being found on one and the same tree.

It is not until the oak is from sixty to a hundred years old that good seeds are obtained from it. Oaks will bear acorns earlier than this, but they are apt to be barren. A curious fact is the tendency to produce large numbers of acorns in a given favourable autumn, and then to bear none, or very few, for three or four years or even longer. The twisted, 'gnarled' character of old oaks is well known, and the remarkably crooked branches are very conspicuous in advanced age and in winter (Plate II.). The bark is also very rugged in the case of ancient trees, the natural inequalities due to fissures, &c., being often supplemented by the formation of ' burrs.'

A not inconsiderable tendency to variation is shown by the oak, and foresters distinguish two sub-species and several varieties of what we regard (adopting the opinion of English systematic botanists) as the single species *Quercus Robur*.

Besides forms with less spreading crowns, the species is frequently broken up into two—*Q. pedunculata*, with the female flowers in rather more lax spikes, and the acorns on short stalks, the leaves sessile or nearly so, and not hairy when young; and *Q. sessiliflora*, with more crowded sessile female flowers, and leaves on short petioles and apt to be hairy. Other minute

characters have also been described, but it is admitted
that the forms vary much, and it is very generally con-
ceded that these two geographical race-forms may be
united with even less marked varieties into the one
species *Quercus Robur.*

The amount of timber produced by a sound old oak
is very large, although the annual increment is so remarkably small. This increment goes on increasing
slightly during the first hundred years or so, and
then falls off; but considerable modifications in both
the habit of the tree and in the amount of timber produced annually, result from different conditions. Trees
grown in closely-planted preserves, for instance, shoot
up to great heights, and develop tall, straight trunks
with few or no branches, and considerable skill in the
forester's art is practised in removing the proper number
of trees at the proper time, to let in the light and air
necessary to cause the maximum production of straight
timber.

Oaks growing in the open air are much shorter,
more branched and spreading, and form the peculiar
dense, twisted timber once so valuable for ship-building
purposes. Such exposed trees, other things being equal,
develop fruit and fertile seeds thirty or forty years sooner
than those growing in closed plantations.

The timber itself is remarkable for combining so
many valuable properties. It is not that oak timber is
the heaviest, the toughest, the most beautiful, &c., of
known woods, but it is because it combines a good

THE OAK IN WINTER (*Rossmässler*).

proportion of weight, toughness, durability, and other qualities that it is so valuable for so many purposes. The richness of the cortex in tannin warranted the growing of young oaks at one time for the bark alone, and the value of the acorns for feeding swine has been immense in some districts.

CHAPTER II

WHEN the acorns are falling in showers from the oaks in October and November, everybody knows that each of the polished, leather-brown, long, egg-shaped bodies tumbles out from a cup-like, scaly investment which surrounded its lower third at the broader end. Perhaps everybody would not be certain as to whether the detached acorn is a seed or a fruit, so I anticipate the difficulty by stating at the outset that the acorn is the fruit of the oak, and contains the seed within its brown shell, and I propose to commence our studies by examining an acorn, deferring the explanation of some minute details of structure until we come to trace the origin of the fruit and seed in the flower.

The average size of the fruit is about 15 to 20 mm., or nearly three-quarters of an inch, long, by 8 to 10 mm., or nearly one-third of an inch, broad at the middle of its length; the end inserted in the cup or *cupule* is broad and nearly flat, and marked by a large circular scar (fig. 2, *s*) denoting the surface of attachment to the cupule. This scar is rough, and exhibits a number

of small points which have resulted from the breaking
of some extremely delicate groups of minute pipes,

FIG. 1.—Sprigs of oak, showing the habit and the arrangement of
the acorns, &c., in September. (After Kotschy.)

called vascular bundles, which placed the acorn in communication with the cup and the tree previous to the

ripening of the former. At the more pointed free end
of the acorn is a queer little knob, which is hard and
dry, and represents the mummified remains of what was
the stigma of the flower, and which lost its importance
several months previously, after receiving the pollen.

The outer hard coat of the acorn is a tough, leather-
brown, polished skin, with fine longitudinal lines on it,
and it forms the outer portion of the true covering of
the fruit, called the *pericarp* (fig. 2, *p*). On removing it
we find a thin, papery membrane inside, adhering partly
to the above coat and partly to the seed inside. This
thin, shrivelled, papery membrane is the inner part of
the pericarp, and the details of structure to be found
in these layers may be passed over for the present with
the remark that they are no longer living structures,
but exist simply as protective coverings for the seed
inside.

The centre of the acorn is occupied more or less
entirely by a hard brown body—the seed—which usually
rattles about loosely on shaking the ripe fruit, but
which was previously attached definitely at the broad
end. A similar series of changes to those which brought
about the separation of the acorn from the cup—
namely, the shrivelling up of the tiny connecting
cords, &c.—also caused the separation of the seed from
the pericarp, and we may regard the former as a distinct body.

Its shape is nearly the same as that of the acorn in
which it loosely fits, and it is usually closely covered with

a thin, brown, wrinkled, papery membrane, which is its
own coat—the seed-coat, or *testa* (fig. 2, *t*). The extent
to which the testa remains adherent to the seed, or to the
inner coat of the pericarp, and both together to the
harder outer coat of the pericarp, need not be commented
upon further than to say that differences in this respect

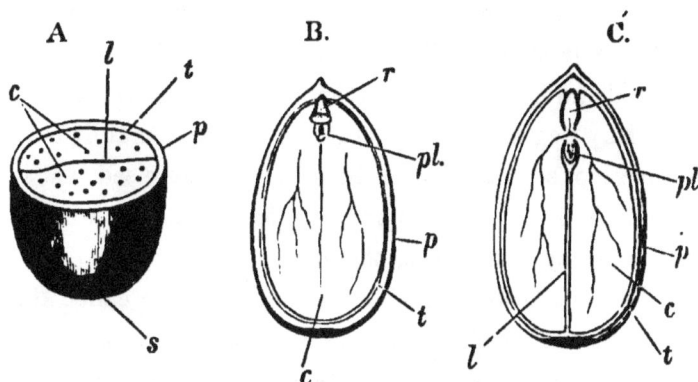

FIG. 2.—Sections of acorns in three planes at right angles to one
another. A, transverse; B, longitudinal in the plane of the cotyledons (*l*); C, longitudinal across the plane of the cotyledons; *c*,
cotyledons; *t*, testa; *p*, pericarp; *s*, scar, and *r*, radicle; *pl*,
plumule. The radicle, plumule, and cotyledons together constitute the embryo. The embryonic tissue is at *r* and *pl*. The dots
in A, and the delicate veins in B and C are the vascular bundles.

are found according to the completeness and ripeness
of the acorn.

Enveloped in its testa and in the pericarp, then,
we find the long acorn-shaped seed, which seems at
first to be a mere horn-like mass without parts. This
is not the case, however, as may easily be observed by
cutting the mass across, or, better still, by first soaking
it in water for some hours; it will then be found that

the egg-shaped body consists chiefly of two longitudinal halves, separated by a median plane which runs through the acorn from top to bottom. These two halves, lying face to face so closely that it requires the above manipulation to enable us to detect the plane of separation (fig. 2, *l*), are not completely independent, however; at a point near the narrower end each of them is attached to the side of a small peg-shaped body, with a conical pointed end turned towards the narrow end of the acorn. This tiny peg-shaped structure is so small that it may be overlooked unless some little care is exercised, but if the hard masses are completely torn apart it will be carried away with one of them.

The two large plano-convex structures are called the *cotyledons*, or seed-leaves (fig. 2, *c*) and they, together with the small peg-shaped body, constitute the *embryo* of the oak. The peg-shaped body presents two ends which project slightly between the two cotyledons beyond the points of attachment to them; the larger of these ends has the shape of a conical bullet, and is directed so that its tip lies in the point of the narrower part of the acorn, the other, and much smaller end, is turned towards the broader extremity of the acorn. The larger, bullet-shaped portion is termed the *radicle* (fig. 2, *r*), and will become the primary root of the oak-plant; the smaller, opposite end is the embryo bud, and is termed the *plumule* (fig. 2, *pl*), and it is destined to develop into the stem and leaves of the oak. If the observer takes the trouble to carefully separate the two large cotyledons, without tearing them

away from the structures just described, he will find that
each is attached by a minute stalk to a sort of ridge just
beneath the tiny plumule; this ridge is sometimes termed
the *collar*. He will also see that the plumule and radicle
fit closely into a cavity formed by the two cotyledons,
and so do not interfere with the very close fitting of
their two flat faces.

Summing up these essential features of the structure
of the ripe acorn and its contents, we find that the
fruit contains within its pericarp (which is a more or less
complex series of layers of which the outermost is hard)
the seed; that this seed comprises a membranous testa
enclosing an embryo; and that the embryo is composed
of two huge cotyledons, a minute radicle, and a still
more minute plumule; and that the tip of the radicle
is turned towards the pointed end of the acorn, lying
just inside the membranes.

Leaving the details of structure of the membranes
until a later period, when we trace their development
from the flower, I must devote some paragraphs to a
description of the minute anatomy and the contents of
the embryo as found in the ripe acorn, so that the
process of germination may be more intelligible.

Thin sections of any portion of the embryo placed
under the microscope show that it consists almost
entirely of polygonal chambers or cells, with very thin
membranous walls, and densely filled with certain granule-
like contents.   These polygonal cells have not their own
independent walls, but the wall which divides any two of

them belongs as much to one as to the other, and only here and there do we find a minute opening between three or more cells at the corners, and produced by the partial splitting of the thin wall. We may, if we like, regard the whole embryo as a single mass of material cut up into chambers by means of partition walls, which have a tendency to split a little here and there, much as one could split a piece of pasteboard by inserting a paper-knife between the layers composing it; what we must *not* do, is to suppose that these cells are so many separate chambers which have been brought into juxta-position. In other words, the cell-wall separating any two of the chambers is in its origin a whole, common to both chambers, and the plane which may be supposed to divide the limits of each is imaginary only.

I have said that the embryo consists almost entirely of this mass of polygonal, thin-walled cells, and such is called *fundamental tissue*; but here and there, in very much smaller proportion, we shall find other structures. Surrounding the whole of the embryo, and following every dip and projection of its contours, will be found a single layer of cells of a flattened, tabular shape, and fitting close together so as to constitute a delicate membrane or skin over the whole embryo; this outer layer of the young plant is called the *epidermis*.

Whenever the cotyledons, or the radicle, or plumule are cut across transversely to their length, there are visible certain very minute specks, which are the cut surfaces of extremely delicate strands or cords of relatively very long and very narrow cells, the minute structure of which we will not now stay to investigate, but simply mention that these extremely fine cords, running in the main longitudinally through the embryo, are termed 'vascular bundles' (fig. 2, A).   It may be shown that there is one set of them running up the central part of the radicle, starting from just beneath its tip, and that these pass into the two cotyledons, and there branch and run in long strands towards the ends of the latter.

The three sets of structures which have been referred to are called ' tissues,' and although they are still in a very young and undeveloped condition we may say that the embryo consists essentially of a large amount of thin-walled cell-tissue, of different ages, which is limited by an epidermal tissue and traversed by vascular tissue. At the tips of the radicle and plumule the cell-tissue is in a peculiar and young condition, and is known as *embryonic tissue*.

As regards the contents and functions of these tissues, the following remarks may suffice for the present.   The polygonal cells of the fundamental tissue of the cotyledons are crowded with numerous brilliant starch grains, of an oval shape and pearly lustre, and these lie embedded in a sort of matrix consisting chiefly of proteids and tannin, together with small quantities of fatty substances.

In each cell there is a small quantity of protoplasm and a nucleus, but this latter is only to be detected with difficulty.   Certain of the cells contain a dark-brown

C

pigment, composed of substances of the nature of
tannin; and small quantities of a peculiar kind of sugar,
called *Quercite*, are also found in the cells, together with
a bitter substance.

In the main, the above are stored up in the thin-
walled parenchyma cells as reserve materials, intended to
supply the growing embryo or seedling with nutritious
food; the starch grains are just so many packets of a
food substance containing carbon, hydrogen, and oxygen
in certain proportions; the proteids are similarly a supply
of nitrogenous food, and minute but necessary quantities of certain mineral salts are mixed with these. The
vascular bundles are practically pipes or conduits which
will convey these materials from the cotyledons to the
radicle and plumule as soon as germination begins, and
I shall say no more of them here, beyond noting that each
strand consists chiefly of a few very minute vessels and
sieve-tubes. The young epidermis takes no part either
in storing or in conducting the food substances; it is
simply a covering tissue, and will go on extending as
the seedling develops a larger and larger surface.

We are now in a position to inquire into what takes
place when the acorn is put into the soil and allowed to
germinate. In nature it usually lies buried among the
decaying leaves on the ground during the winter, and
it may even remain for nearly a year without any conspicuous change; and in any case it requires a period
of rest before the presence of the oxygen of the air and
the moisture of the soil are effective in making it ger-

minate—a fact which suggests that some profound mole-
cular or chemical changes have to be completed in the
living substance of the cells before further activity is
possible. We have other reasons for believing that
this is so, and that, until certain ferments have been
prepared in the cells, their protoplasm is unable to make
use of the food materials, and consequently unable to
initiate the changes necessary for growth.

Sooner or later, however, and usually as the temperature rises in spring, the embryo in the acorn absorbs
water and oxygen, and swells, and the little radicle elongates and drives its tip through the ruptured investments
at the thin end of the acorn, and at once turns downward,
and plunges slowly into the soil (fig. 3). This peculiarity of turning downwards is so marked that it manifests
itself no matter in what position the acorn lies, and it
is obviously of advantage to the plant that the radicle
should thus emerge first, and turn away from the light,
and grow as quickly as possible towards the centre of
the earth, because it thus establishes a first hold on the
soil, in readiness to absorb water and dissolve mineral
substances by the time the leaves open and require
them.

The two cotyledons remain enclosed in the coats of
the acorn, and are not lifted up into the air; the developing root obtains its food materials from the stores
in the cells of the cotyledons, as do all the parts of the
young seedling at this period. In fact, these stores in
the cotyledons contribute to the support of the baby

c 2

plant for many months, and even two years may elapse
before they are entirely exhausted.

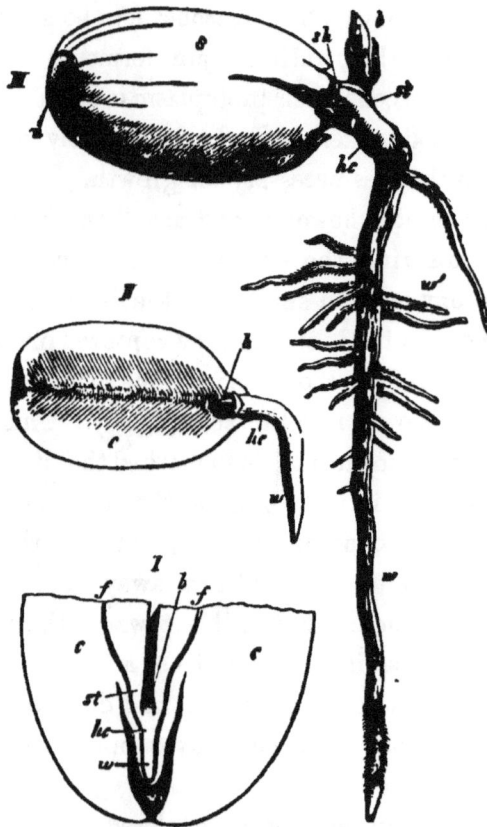

FIG. 3.—I. Longitudinal section through the posterior half of the
embryo, in a plane at right angles to the plane of separation between the cotyledons (slightly magnified). II. Germinating
embryo, with one cotyledon removed. III. Acorn in an advanced
stage of germination. *a*, the scar; *s*, pericarp; *sh*, testa; *b*,
plumule; *st*, petioles of cotyledons, from between which the
plumule, *b*, emerges; *hc*, hypocotyl; *c*, cotyledons; *f*, vascular
bundles; *w*, radicle (primary root); *w'*, secondary roots. Root-
hairs are seen covering the latter and the anterior part of the
primary root in III. (After Sachs.)

When the elongated radicle, or primary root, has attained a length of two or three inches in the soil, and its tip is steadily plunging with a very slight rocking movement deeper and deeper into the earth, the little plumule emerges from between the very short stalks of the cotyledons (fig. 3, *st*), which elongate and separate to allow of its exit, and grows erect into the light and air above ground.   It will be understood that this plumule also is living at the expense of the food stores in the cotyledons, the dissolved substances passing up into it through the tiny vascular bundles and cells, as they have all along been passing down to the growing root through the similar channels in its tissues.

The plumule—or, as we must now call it, primary shoot—differs from the root not only in its more tardy growth at first, but also in its habit of growing away from the centre of gravitation of the earth and into the light and air ; and here, again, we have obviously adaptations which are of advantage to the plant, which would soon be top-heavy, moreover, if the shoot were far developed before the root had established a hold-fast in the soil.

The little oak shoot is for some time apparently devoid of leaves (fig. 4), but a careful examination shows that as it elongates it bears a few small scattered scales, like tiny membranes, each of which has a very minute bud in its axil.   When the primary shoot has attained a length of about three inches there are usually two of these small scale-leaves placed nearly opposite one another close to the tip, and a little longer and narrower than those lower down on the shoot; from between these two linear structures the first true green foliage leaf of the oak arises, its short stalk being flanked by them. This

first leaf is small, but the tip of the shoot goes on elongating and throwing out others and larger ones, until by the end of the summer there are about four to six leaves formed, each with its minute stalk flanked by a pair of tiny linear scales ('stipules,' as they are called) like those referred to above.

Each of the green leaves arises from a point on the young stem which is a little higher, and more to one side, than that from which the lowermost one springs; hence a line joining the points of insertion of the successive leaves describes an open spiral round the shoot axis—*i.e.* the stem—and this of such a kind that when the spiral comes to the sixth leaf upwards it is vertically above the first or oldest leaf from which we started, and has passed twice round the stem.

FIG. 4. — Germinating acorn, showing the manner of emergence of the primary shoot, and the first scales (stipules) on the latter. (After Rossmässler.)

At the end of this first year, which we may term

the period of germination, the young oak-plant or seedling has a primary root some twelve to eighteen inches long, and with numerous shorter, spreading side rootlets, and a shoot from six to eight inches high, bearing five or six leaves as described, and terminating in a small ovoid bud (figs. 3 and 4). The whole shoot is clothed with numerous very fine soft hairs, and there are also numerous fine root-hairs on the roots, and clinging to the particles of soil. The tip of each root is protected by a thin colourless cap—the root-cap—the description of which we defer for the present.

About May, in the second year, each of the young roots is elongating in the soil and putting forth new root-hairs and rootlets, while the older roots are thickening and becoming harder and covered with cork; and each of the buds in the axils of the last year's leaves begins to shoot out into a branch, bearing new leaves in its turn, while the bud at the end of the shoot elongates and lengthens the primary stem, the older parts of which are also becoming thicker and clothed with cork. And so the seedling develops into an oak-plant, each year becoming larger and more complex, until it reaches the stage of the sapling, and eventually becomes a tree.

CHAPTER III

THE SEEDLING AND YOUNG PLANT

BEFORE proceeding to describe the further growth and development of the seedling, it will be well to examine its structure in this comparatively simple stage, in order to obtain points of view for our studies at a later period.   For many reasons it is advantageous to begin with the root-system.   If we cut a neat section accurately transverse to the long axis of the root, and a few millimetres behind its tip, the following parts may be discerned with the aid of a good lens, or a microscope, on the flat face of the almost colourless section.   A circular area of greyish cells occupies the centre—this is called the axis cylinder of the young root (fig. 5, A, a). Surrounding this is a wide margin of larger cells, forming a sort of sheathing cylinder to this axial one, and termed the *root-cortex*.   The superficial layer of cells of this root-cortex has been distinguished as a special tissue, like an epidermis, and as it is the layer which alone produces the root-hairs, we may conveniently regard it as worthy of distinction as the piliferous layer (fig. 5, e).

Similar thin sections a little nearer the tip of the

root would show a more or less loose sheath of cells in
addition to and outside this piliferous layer. This is the
root-cap, which is a thimble-shaped sheath of looser cells

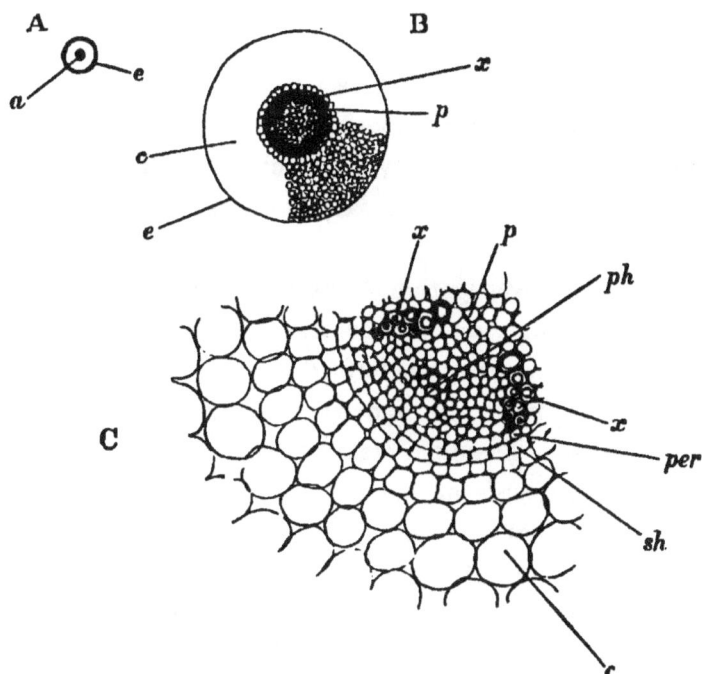

FIG. 5.—A. Transverse section of young root under a lens, showing
the axis-cylinder, *a*; epidermis or piliferous layer, *e*; and the
cortex between. B. The same more highly magnified: *c*, cortex;
p, phloëm; *x*, xylem. C. A portion still more highly magnified:
ph, phloëm; *p*, pith; *per*, pericycle; *sh*, sheath (endodermis);
other letters as before.

covering the tip of the root as a thimble covers the end
of the finger, only we must imagine the extreme tip of
the finger organically connected with the inside of the
cap to make the analogy suitable (see fig. 6).   The rest

of the section would be much as before, excepting that the distinction between the axial cylinder and the root-cortex would be less marked.

Now contrast a section cut a couple of inches or so away from the tip, in the region where the root-hairs are well developed. Here we find the axial cylinder much more strongly marked than before, and the piliferous layer is very clearly distinguished by the fact that it gives off the root-hairs, each hair arising from one of its cells.

A little investigation shows that the axial cylinder is thus strongly marked because certain dark-looking structures have now been formed just inside its boundary —*i.e.* just inside the line which delimits it from the root-cortex. These dark structures are the sections of several fine cords or bundles, called vascular bundles, which can here be traced up and down in the root. As the section shows, these bundles are arranged at approximately equal distances in a cylinder; they form the vascular system of the root, and they always run along the region just inside the outer boundary of the axis-cylinder (fig. 5, B, *p* and *x*).

If we compare our successive transverse sections, and cut others at various levels along the young root, it will be clear that, as we pass from the tip of the root to parts further behind, certain changes must be going on, which result first in the definite marking out of the axial cylinder, and then in the development of these vascular bundles and of other parts we will not describe in detail.

If, in addition to these successive transverse sections, we examine a carefully prepared longitudinal section, cut so as to pass accurately through the median plane of the root, the comparison not only establishes the above conclusion, but it enables us to be certain of yet other facts (fig. 6). Such a section shows the root-cap covering the tip as a thimble the end of the finger, and the rim of this root-cap is evidently fraying away behind; the cells of which it is composed die and slough off as the root pushes its way between the abrading particles of soil. Obviously this loss of worn-out tissue must be made good in some way, and closer examination shows how this occurs. The extreme tip of the root proper fits closely into the cap, and evidently adds cells to the inside of the latter, and thus replaces the old ones which are worn away. At this true tip of the root, moreover, we make another discovery—namely, that all the cells are there *alike* in shape, size,

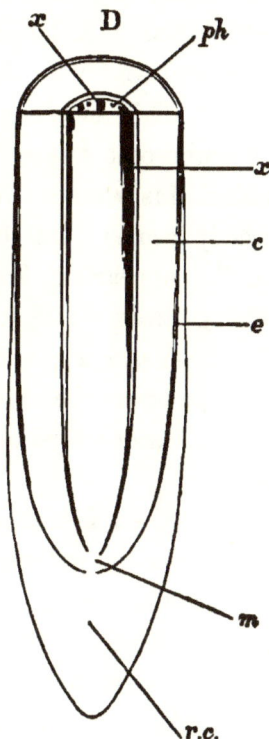

Fig. 6 —Diagrammatic section through the end of the root of the oak. *c*, root-cortex; *e*, piliferous layer; *rc*, root-cap; *m*, the true embryonic tissue (so-called 'growing-point'); *ph*, phloëm; *x*, xylem.

and other peculiarities; and if we could take a transverse section exactly at this place we should see no
differentiation into axial cylinder and root-cortex, &c.
—the small circular mass would consist of cells all
alike, and with very thin walls and full of dense protoplasm. This undifferentiated formative tissue is called
the embryonic tissue of the root (fig. 6, *m*). A little
behind this we see the axis-cylinder and root-cortex
already formed; still further away we see the vascular
bundles appearing, first as very thin cords, and then
getting stronger and stronger as we recede from the tip
(fig. 6, *ph* and *x*); and similarly we trace the gradual
development of the other parts in acropetal succession—
i.e. the nearer we go to the apex the younger the parts
are.

Now, there is a conclusion of some importance to be
drawn from the putting together of these facts—namely,
that all the structures found between the embryonic
tissue at the tip of the root and the place where the root
joins the stem have been gradually formed from the
embryonic tissue in acropetal succession. We may
picture this by marking a given level on the root,
some distance away from the tip, where the axis-cylinder
is sharply marked and has well developed vascular bundles, the root-cortex is distinct, and the piliferous layer
bears root-hairs, and remembering that so many days or
weeks ago this very spot was in the then growing-point,
and consisted of embryonic tissue with the cells all alike.
Or we may put it in a different way thus: the present

growing-point consists of embryonic cells all alike; in a few days some of these cells will have changed into constituents of the axis-cylinder and cortex, and subsequently some of them will give rise to vascular bundles, &c. Not all, however, and it is necessary to understand that as the embryonic tissue moves onwards and leaves the structures referred to in its wake, it does so by producing new embryonic cells in front—*i.e.* between the present ones and the root-cap.

We must now look a little more closely into the structure of the axial cylinder, at a level a little behind the region where the root-hairs are produced on the piliferous layer.

A thin transverse section in this region shows that the root-hairs have all died away, and the walls of the cells of the piliferous layer are becoming discoloured, being, in fact, converted into a brown, cork-like substance impervious to moisture, or nearly so; consequently the piliferous layer is no longer absorptive, and it will soon be thrown off, as we shall see.

The cortex offers little to notice, except that its cells are being passively stretched or compressed by the growth and processes going on in the axial cylinder, and it is this cylinder that attracts our special attention, and several points not noticed before must now be examined in some detail.

In the first place, the cylinder is demarcated off from the cortex by a single layer of cells shaped like bricks, and with a sort of black dot on the radial walls;

this is called the *endodermis*, and may be regarded as
a sheath limiting what belongs to the axis-cylinder (fig.
5, C, *sh*).   Inside this endodermis are about two rows
of thin-walled cells full of protoplasm, and forming a
continuous layer beneath the endodermis.   This layer is
termed the *pericycle* (fig. 5, C, *per*), and it is a very
important structure, because its cells give rise, by repeated divisions, to the lateral rootlets, which then
grow out and burst their way through the endodermis,
cortex, and piliferous layer, and so reach the soil.   It is,
of course, necessary to bear in mind that the endodermis
and pericycle are concentric cylinders superposed on
the axis of the root, as it were, and only appear as rings
on the transverse section.

Inside the pericycle are arranged the vascular
bundles, and we shall have to devote a few words of explanation to these remarkable and somewhat complex
structures.

The section shows that there are about ten alternating groups of tissue constituting these bundles, and
again the reader must bear in mind that each group is
the transverse section of a long cord running up and
down the root.   Of these groups five are much more
conspicuous than the other five, because they consist
chiefly of more or less polygonal openings with firm,
dark contours.   These are the xylem vessels of the vascular bundles (fig. 5, C, *x*), and we must note the following
facts about them :—In the first place, they are smaller
near the pericycle than they are nearer the centre of

the axial cylinder, and the comparison of numerous transverse sections at different levels of the root would prove that the smallest vessels are the first to develop; whence we learn two facts—namely, that the xylem vessels of the young root are developed in centripetal order, and that the later ones have a larger calibre than those formed earlier.

If longitudinal sections are compared with these transverse ones—and I may here observe that it is only by means of numerous such comparisons that these matters have been gradually discovered—it is found that each vessel is a long tube, usually containing air and water when complete, the lateral walls of which are curiously and beautifully marked with characteristic thick and thin ornamentation. It must suffice here to say that the small, outer, first-formed vessels are marked with a spiral thickening, reminding one of caoutchouc gas-tubing kept open by means of a spiral wire inside; while the larger ones, developed later, usually have numerous small pits on their walls, reminding one of mouths, and the structure of which is very curious. Consequently these groups of xylem vessels are said to consist of spiral and pitted vessels, and their chief function is to convey water up the root to the stem (*cf.* fig. 16). Packed in between these vessels are certain cells known as the wood-cells.

Returning to the transverse section, we saw that between each xylem group described above there is a group of structures differing from the latter in their less

distinct outlines; these alternate groups are known as
phloëm, and we may shortly examine the elements of
which they are composed, as before, by comparing
sections of various kinds.

Here, again, we find the chief structures in the phloëm
are also vessels—*i.e.* long, tubular organs—but very different in detail from the vessels of the xylem.

In the first place, their walls are thin and soft, and
composed of the unaltered cellulose which is so characteristic of young cells (instead of being hard like the
lignified walls of the xylem vessels); then, again, they
contain protoplasm and other organised cell contents,
instead of merely air and water. Finally, they are not
so completely tubular as the typical xylem vessels are,
because the transverse septa of the constituent cells are
not absorbed, but are merely pierced by fine strands of
protoplasm, and therefore look like sieves when viewed
from above—whence the name 'sieve-tubes.' In the
phloëm also we find cells—phloëm-cells—packed in
between the sieve-tubes.

If we shortly summarise the above we find that the
root consists of an axis-cylinder surrounded by a cortex
and the piliferous layer. At the tip the whole is
covered by the root-cap, which is organically connected
with the embryonic tissue which forms all these structures. The axis-cylinder is somewhat complex; it is
sheathed by the endodermis and the pericycle, the
latter of which gives origin to the new rootlets. Inside
the pericycle are the vascular bundles running up and

FIG. 7.—Portion of young growing ends of more advanced
root, with numerous rootlets. Some of the latter are much
branched into tuft-like collections, *m*; these form the
so-called *Mycorhiza*. Natural size.

D

down as separate, alternate cords of xylem and phloëm ;
the xylem consists of vessels and cells, the former
developed centripetally, while the phloëm consists of
sieve-tubes and cells. Any cell-tissue which may lie in
the centre of the axial cylinder, and surrounded by the
vascular bundles, corresponds, in popular language, to
pith ; any that runs between the bundles corresponds
to medullary rays.

We now turn to the root as a whole, and examine
its behaviour in the soil as the young seedling develops
further, and in the light of the above anatomical
facts.

Although the root-system of the young plant is
regularly constituted of a series of lateral rootlets
springing from the primary root, the orderly arrangement is soon disturbed when the tertiary and other
rootlets begin to develop from the secondary rootlets ;
moreover, as the age of the tree increases, the tendency
to irregularity is increased owing to the production of
rootlets of the higher orders at different places, thus
interfering with the acropetal succession of the younger
rootlets.

At first the root-system is especially engaged in
boring into the soil, and provided the latter is sufficiently deep and otherwise suitable, the tap-root will go
down a foot or more in the first year. As the roots
thicken they exhibit considerable plasticity, as is especially evinced on rocky ground, where the older roots
may often be found in cracks in the rocks, so com-

pressed that they form mere flattened sheets many times broader than they are thick (fig. 8).

It has already been mentioned that the tip of the young primary root circumnutates, and Darwin also found that the tip of the radicle is extremely sensitive to the irritation of small bodies in contact with it. It is also positively geotropic, directing itself vertically downwards if the partially grown radicle is laid horizontally; and it may be assumed from the behaviour of other plants of the same kind that the tip of the radicle is negatively heliotropic—*i.e.* it turns away from the source of light. Whether it is also sensitive to differences in the degree of moisture on different sides (hydrotropic), or to differ-

FIG. 8.—Portion of an older root of an oak, which had penetrated while young between two pieces of hard rock, and had to adapt its form accordingly as it thickened. (After Döbner.)

D 2

ences of temperature (thermotropic), is not known, but it may be inferred that such is the case; nor do we know whether it is affected by electric currents in the earth.

The root of the oak, speaking generally, is a typical root in the following respects. It consists, as we have seen, of a primary or tap-root which develops secondary or lateral roots in acropetal succession, and these in their turn produce rootlets of a higher order. These secondary, tertiary, &c., rootlets arise endogenously, taking origin from the pericycle at the periphery of the strand of vascular bundles which traverse the central axis, and then bursting through the cortex to the exterior. The primary root, as well as the rootlets of all orders, are provided with a root-cap at the tips, and they all agree in being devoid of chlorophyll or stomata. From the outer layer of cells—the piliferous layer, corresponding to an epidermis—root-hairs are developed at some little distance behind the root-cap, and these superficial cellular outgrowths also arise in acropetal succession, the older ones behind dying off as the younger ones arise further forwards. If we bear in mind all that has been shortly stated above, it will be very easy to figure the behaviour of the root-system as it penetrates the ground, and the following short description of the biology of the root may render the matter clear. When the radicle commences to bore down into the soil it puts forth a large number of root-hairs from the parts a few millimetres behind the tip, and these attach themselves to the

particles of soil and supply points of resistance; the tip
of the radicle is protected by the slippery root-cap, and
it must be borne in mind that the embryonic tissue of the
growing-point consists of thin-walled cells full of relatively stiff protoplasm with very little water.   Hence
the growing-point is a firm body.   The most active
growth of the root takes place at a region several millimetres behind the root-cap, between it and the fixed
point above referred to; hence the apex of the root is
really driven into the ground between the particles of
rock, &c., of which the latter is composed.   This driving
in is aided by the negative heliotropism, the positive
geotropism, the circumnutation, and other irritabilities
of the apical portions of the root, and it bores its way
several centimetres downwards. As it lengthens—by the
addition of cells produced by the division of those of the
embryonic tissue, and by their successive elongation—
the older parts behind go on producing root-hairs, and
thus a vertical cylinder of soil around the primary root
is gradually laid under contribution for water containing dissolved salts, &c.   In those parts of the root which
are behind the growing region no further elongation
occurs; hence the tips of the lateral rootlets (which have
been developing in the pericycle at the circumference of
the axial cylinder of vascular bundles) can now safely
break through the cortex and extend themselves in the
same manner from the parent root as a fixed base,
without danger of being broken off by the elongation
of the growing parts.   Each of these secondary rootlets

grows out at an obtuse angle from the primary root, and not vertically downwards, and as it does so a similar wave of root-hairs is developed along it; thus a series of nearly horizontal radiating cylinders of soil are placed under contribution as before. Then the secondary rootlets emit tertiary rootlets in all directions—these and the rootlets of a higher order growing without any particular reference to the direction of gravitation, light, &c.—and so place successive cylinders of soil in all directions under contribution as before. By this time, however, the symmetry of the root-system is being disturbed because some of the rootlets meet with stones or other obstacles, others get dried up or frozen, or gnawed off or otherwise injured, and the varying directions in which new growths start and in which the resistances are least, influence the very various shapes of the tangled mass of roots now permeating the soil in all directions.

These roots supply the ever-increasing needs for water of the shoot-system, the leaf-surface of which is becoming larger and larger, and as the greater volume of water from the gathering rootlets has all to enter the stem *via* the upper part of the main root, we are not surprised to find that the latter thickens, as does the stem; and so with all the older roots—they no longer act as absorbing roots, but become merely larger and larger channels for water, and girder-like supporting organs.

CHAPTER IV

THE SEEDLING AND YOUNG PLANT (*continued*)

ITS SHOOT-SYSTEM—DISTRIBUTION OF THE TISSUES

I NOW proceed to describe the chief features of importance in the structure of the shoot of the young oak-
plant, premising that many of the remarks may here be
curtailed in view of the facts already learnt in connection with the root. The first object will be to bring
out the differences in the shoot as contrasted with the
root, and first we may examine the structure by means
of transverse sections as before. The shoot consists of
all the structures developed from the plumule.

Such sections show that we have here also various
definitely grouped tissues, of which we may conveniently
distinguish three systems. A series of vascular bundles
grouped in a close ring constitutes one of these systems,
another is represented by a single layer of cells at
the periphery of the section, and this is called the
epidermis, and the remainder of the section composes
the third system, often termed the fundamental tissue,
and divided arbitrarily into three regions—the pith, the
cortex, and the primary medullary rays (fig. 9). The

chief points of difference from the root are that the
xylem and phloëm of these vascular bundles of the stem
do not alternate on the section, as they did in the root,
but the phloëm of each bundle is on the same radius as
the xylem ; and that there is no pericycle, for branches

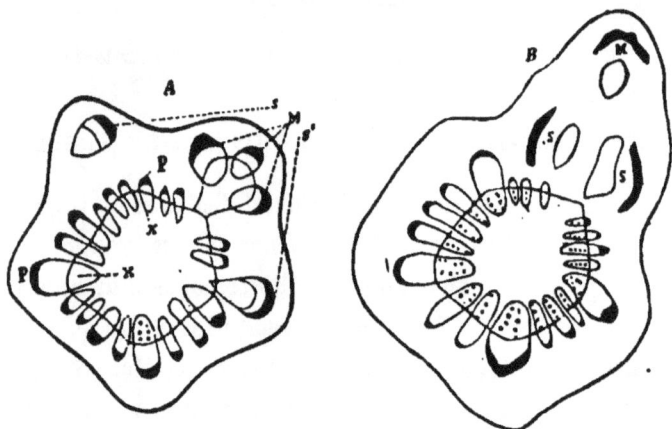

FIG. 9.—Transverse sections through very young twigs of
oak, showing the vascular bundles of the stem (P and X),
arranged in a ring round the pith, and joined by the
cambium ring—the fine line passing through the bundles ; M and *s* the vascular bundles passing down from
the leaves, M the median bundles, and *s* the lateral
bundles. The external outline is the epidermis ; the
letters P, P stand in the primary cortex ; the letters X, x
stand in the pith ; the primary medullary rays separate
the bundles. (After Müller).

are not developed endogenously as rootlets are.   Then
there are some important differences in the mode of
origin of these vascular bundles in space.   We saw that
in the root the first-formed spiral vessels are developed
at the outer parts of the axis-cylinder, nearest the
cortex, and the succeeding vessels are formed in centri-

petal order from these points. In the young stem the
exact converse occurs—the first spiral vessels arise near
the centre of the stem, and development proceeds cen-
trifugally from the first. We may begin our study of
the shoot by tracing the course of the vascular bundles,
which, it must be remembered, are the channels of communication between the water-supply at the roots below
and the leaves and young parts of the shoot above.

If we cut a transverse section of the terminal bud of
the oak, as close to the tip as possible, we shall obtain a
preparation of the young axis consisting entirely of
embryonic tissue, all the cells of which are practically
alike—small, polygonal, thin-walled cells, with large
nuclei and much protoplasm, but without sap-vacuoles ;
these cells are in a state of active division, those in the
interior dividing successively in all planes. Those which
form the peripheral layer, however, are already distinguished by only dividing in the two planes at right
angles to the periphery, and they constitute the primi-
tive epidermis.   There is no structure corresponding
to a root-cap.

Transverse sections a little lower down show differences of the following nature. In the first place the
outline of the section tends to be somewhat pentagonal,
the points of origin of the very young leaves being at
the angles of the pentagon in accordance with their
phyllotaxis—i.e. the order in which the leaves are
arranged on the stem. This is of such a nature that
each leaf stands some distance above and to one side of

its next neighbour below, and if a line be drawn from
the insertion of any one leaf through the points of insertion of those above, it will describe a spiral, and will
eventually come to a leaf standing directly above the
leaf started from. In doing this the spiral line will
pass twice round the stem, and through the points of
insertion of five leaves. This is shortly expressed by $\frac{2}{5}$.

The previously homogeneous embryonic tissue in
the section now shows certain patches of greyer, closer
tissue, arranged round the centre in a peculiar manner;
these are transverse sections of the young vascular
bundles—strands which at present are distinguished
chiefly by the small diameter of their cells, whence the
darker grey appearance.

These strands when young are called procambium
strands. Their cells are distinguished from the other
embryonic cells around by growing more in length and
dividing less frequently across their length, and by
growing less in breadth and dividing more often by
longitudinal walls.

On transverse sections a little lower down there may
be seen a number of elongated and curved patches of
procambium, as shown in fig. 9. On the section it will
be noticed that the larger strands are so arranged that
they enclose a five-angled mass of central tissue (the
pith), the five corners pointing to the angles of the
young stem to which the leaves are attached. At the
corners or ends of the rays just referred to are in some
cases two or three smaller strands.

Now, the important point to apprehend first is that
these strands at the corners (M, *s*) are the strands which
pass directly into the leaves through the petioles, and
it is necessary to be perfectly clear on this subject in
order to understand much of what follows. For instance,
the three strands marked M in fig. 9, A (*mm*, *ms*, and
ms in fig. 10), pass directly into a given leaf, *mm*, in
the middle, flanked by *ms* on either side; but this
group is also accompanied on each side by another strand,
(marked *s*, *s'* in fig. 9, A, and *l*, *l* in fig. 10), so that five
strands may be regarded as contributing to each corner
of the section, the three middle ones running side by
side up the midrib of the leaf and then branching out
in a manner to be described subsequently.

It can be shown, moreover, that the larger curved
strands, occupying the sides of the pentagon, are simply
formed by the union of several of the smaller strands at
different levels.

If, now, successively lower sections are cut of the
very young shoot, and compared, or if the shoot is
softened and dissected, it is possible to make out the
course of these vascular bundle strands lower down;
the course is somewhat complex, but the diagrammatic
sketches in fig. 11 will enable the reader to apprehend
the chief points.

In the first place, the middle strand from a leaf,
mm, passes vertically down in the angle of the young
stem through five internodes (marked by the horizontal
lines), turning to one side and becoming continuous in

the fifth internode with a strand coming off from another
leaf situated at another of the angles at a different level.
The strands which stand next to this median one—one
on each side (*ms*)—at first also pass vertically down
together with it, but at about the second or third internode below they break up into smaller strands, which

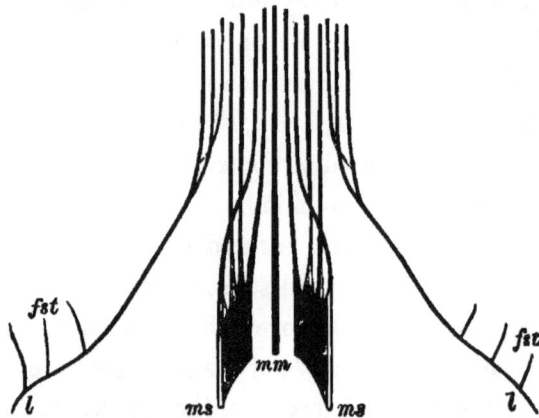

FIG. 10.—Diagram of the course of the bundles M, *s*, and *s'*
of fig. 9, as they pass out of the stem into the base of
the leaf-stalk. *mm* is the median bundle, and *ms*, *ms* its
two companions (M in fig. 9, A); *l, l* are the lateral
bundles *s* and *s'* of fig. 9, A. The small branches *fst* go
into the stipules. (After Frank.)

again join with strands coming from other leaves situated
at other nodes and angles.

If we again compare the figures it will be seen
that the three strands just traced come down in the
angle of the stem, only turning aside lower down—the
median strand *mm*, indeed, running actually in the
angle through five internodes.

To right and left in fig. 10 are seen two strands,

marked *l*, *l*, and these
run chiefly in what
may be called the faces
of the five-angled stem;
only, at the node where
the leaf we are consi-
dering is inserted, they
turn in towards the leaf,
and eventually they run
into the sides of the
petiole of the leaf as
the so-called 'lateral
strands,' or bundles.

Now, observation
shows that these lateral
strands (marked *l*, *l²*, *l³*,
&c., in the diagram,
fig. 11) receive contri-
butions at successive

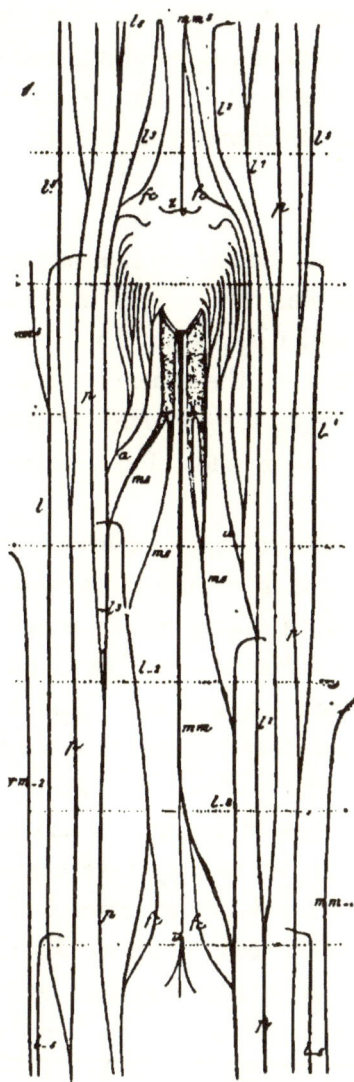

FIG. 11.—Diagram of the
course of the vascular
bundles as they come
down from the leaves into
the stem. The horizontal
dotted lines represent the
levels of successive leaves;
the triangular white area
beneath the upper letter *z*
is the insertion of a leaf.
Each group of bundles
from a leaf, as *mm*, *ms*, *ms*,
&c. (see text), descends into the stem, and joins with the bundles
from other leaves after running through several internodes. The
other letters refer to the bundles from other leaves. (After Frank.)

nodes, and pass down as stronger and stronger strands through about seven internodes, their lower ends losing themselves by joining to others; and in fact the larger bundles seen on the transverse section (fig. 9) are larger because they consist of so many contingents running parallel, or nearly so, down the stem.

It results from this that all the vascular bundles in the stem are simply composed of strands which run into the leaves on the one hand, and down the internodes on the other; and, as further comparison will show, all these bundles are continuous in the stem, since the lower ends of the strands are joined on to other strands.

Moreover, as an examination of the diagrams and figures shows, the main course of these bundles in the stem is approximately parallel—they run side by side down from the leaf insertion through two, three, or more internodes, and only bend aside to any great extent when they pass out into a leaf or to join with others. In the section (fig. 9), for instance, all the little bundles at the angles and outside the ring are cut at levels where they have abandoned the larger bundles and are bending outwards through the cortex to the leaves; lower down we should find them joining to the larger bundles at various levels, and running down with them, just as strands from leaves at higher levels are now conjoined to make up these larger bundles.

The group of vascular bundles which passes into the stem from the insertion of a leaf is spoken of collectively as the 'leaf-trace.' Hence we see the leaf-trace of the oak consists of five bundles —one median, two lateral median, and two lateral—and since the phyllotaxis of the oak is $\frac{2}{5}$, there will be twenty-five bundles in various stages of separation or conjunction coming down in the five internodes between any one leaf and the leaf vertically above it, as well as the parts of bundles from other leaves which are still continuing their course for a short time.

Now, since the main lengths of the course (in the stem) of these bundles is nearly vertically downwards, with slight swerves to one side or another as the strands join, it is obvious that on the transverse section of the stem the bundles will appear arranged in a series round the centre—in fact, they will form on the whole a more or less regular ring of bundles dividing off the pith from the cortical portions of the stem. Even in the very young condition (fig. 9) we see bundles or groups of strands thus surrounding the pith, only the 'ring' which they make is a sinuous one, so that the pith is five-rayed—a characteristic point in the oak. At a slightly later stage, as we shall see, this ring of bundles becomes more nearly circular from the gradual filling up of irregularities.

Before proceeding further it is necessary to make clear one or two other points. Since all the vascular bundles in the oak-stem are bundles which are common to the stem and leaf, they are termed 'common bundles.' We have seen that a given strand or bundle may run for part of its course simply side by side with another and *separate* from it; at other parts of the course the bundles may be *united* with others. In the case of the oak it will be clearly borne in mind that the individual or separate bundles of the leaf-trace pass into the stem at the node of insertion of the given leaf, and then run down side by side at a practically constant distance from the surface of the epidermis on the one hand, and the longitudinal axis of the pith on the other. At different levels below, at or very near nodes, these bundles turn aside laterally—*i.e.* in the tangential plane, and hence, still keeping their mean distance from the epidermis and pith, join with others.

This being understood, it is also obvious that on the whole the collection of vascular bundles in a young branch form a nearly cylindrical trellis-work or meshwork symmetrically disposed between the pith and the cortex, and that the latter (cortex and pith) are in connection through the meshes between the interpectinating and concomitant vascular bundles. These radial connections of the pith and cortex are the primary medullary rays.

It will now be clear why we observe on transverse sections of the young stem taken across an internode the arrangement shown in fig. 9. The vascular bundles are grouped in a ring round the pith, separating it off from the cortex and its covering the epidermis, and with those primary medullary rays which happen to have been cut running between the bundles.

If we now trace the vascular bundles of the leaf-trace in the other direction—that is, up into the leaf—their course is simple enough, as shown in figs. 10 and 11. The five bundles run through the midrib and the stronger lateral ribs to the tips and edges of the leaf, first breaking up into several strands in the petiole and midrib, and then becoming finer and finer as they give off the lateral strands. The median bundle does little more than run directly through the leaf as the midrib, becoming finer and finer as it nears the apex. The two lateral median bundles behave in a somewhat curious way. We have already seen how large and flat they are at the leaf insertion (fig. 10). Soon after entering the petiole they break up into several strands, two of which converge and take a course along the dorsal side of the midrib, thus nearly completing a cylinder of bundles enclosing a pith ; moreover, the xylem portions of these bundles are all turned inwards towards the pith.

The lateral bundles, coming obliquely into the leaf insertion, pass up the midrib side by side with the above, and, like them, break up into parallel strands. Before entering the midrib they give off small bundles (*fst* in fig. 10) to the pair of minute stipules which flank the petiole. As the strands pass along the midribs and chief lateral ribs they interosculate in various degrees, and give off smaller side branches into the mesophyll of the leaf (see Chapter VI.).

The veins which spring from the chief lateral ribs run towards one another and anastomose, giving off

E

smaller veins which form a network in the area included by them. In the neighbourhood of the leaf-margin, however, the smaller veins curve towards one another, and make arches convex towards the margin. In the finer meshes individual minute branches run to the centre of a mesh and end there. Round the extreme edge of the leaf is a single vascular bundle ; this receives small bundles from the above-mentioned arches, and also receives the ends of the midrib and the chief lateral ribs (*cf.* fig. 1).

The vascular bundles of the axillary bud, which will eventually, of course, form a system like that already described on their own account, pass down and join the bundles of the parent axis as follows.

The bundles of each lateral half of the bud (fig. 11, *a a*) pass down together between the bundles of the leaf-trace of the leaf from whose axil the bud arises, and the next lateral bundles of the stem with which the leaf-trace bundles are conjoined; the common strand formed by the bundles of each side of the bud then joins with a bundle coming down from another leaf. A few of the strands may also join to the bundles of the leaf-trace itself.

At the back or top side of the bud—*i.e.* the side next the stem which bears it—a few vascular bundles pass from the bud to the nearest strand (fig. 11, *z*); this is the middle strand coming down from the leaf vertically above the bud—*i.e.* the sixth leaf up the stem. Knowing this, we of course know how the branch is joined to the stem. Several other small strands also are formed, as at z, to complete the filling up of the gap, and these may be called completing bundles. These connecting and completing bundles enable the young shoot as it develops from the bud to enclose its own pith in a cylinder of vascular tissue continuous with that of the parent shoot.

We thus see that the vascular bundles form a connected system in the leaves, buds (*i.e.* young branches), and stem, and it only remains to add that they are joined below to those of the root-system, with which, in fact, they took origin in the very young embryo. Hence, if we were to remove the whole of the softer tissues of the oak-plant, we should have a model of it left in the form of a more or less open basket-work of vascular bundles. It is necessary to bear this in mind, as some important conclusions follow from it subsequently.

CHAPTER V

THE SEEDLING AND YOUNG PLANT (*continued*)

STRUCTURE OF THE VASCULAR TISSUES, &c.

BEFORE plunging into the intricacies of the vascular
bundles it will be well to obtain some idea of the
general plan of structure which they present on transverse section (fig. 9). As already seen, each of the bundles
of the ring consists of a xylem portion on the side next
the centre of the stem, and a phloëm portion on the side
next the periphery, and these portions are separated
by the cambium layer. The tissue in the centre of the
stem, and surrounded by the ring of bundles, is called
the pith; the tissue outside the ring, and between it
and the epidermis, is called the cortex; and the tissue
left between the bundles is termed the primary medullary rays (fig. 9).

It will, of course, be remembered that the term
'ring,' as used above, always expresses the fact that a
cylinder is here viewed in section. Now, the cambium
of the individual bundles soon unites across the primary
medullary rays, and thus a complete hollow cylinder of

FIG. 12.—Transverse section of young stem, showing primary
vascular bundles, &c., highly magnified. *a* and *b*, the
pith ; *c*, primary cortex ; *i*, epidermis ; *h*, periderm (cork);
g, collenchyma. Two complete primary vascular bundles,
and parts of two others, are shown, separated by the
primary medullary rays. *r*, spiral vessels (protoxylem);
k, bast-fibres (protophloëm); *n, m*, cambium, separating
the phloëm from the xylem; *p*, wood-parenchyma.
Secondary medullary rays are seen in the bundles, as
also are pitted vessels of different sizes. (Th. Hartig.)

cambium is formed throughout the stem, and, as we shall see later, throughout the root also. For the present it must suffice to notice that the cells of this cambium cylinder go on developing into new xylem, or phloëm, or medullary rays, according to position and circumstances; meanwhile we are only concerned with the vascular bundles of the young shoot.

On the transverse section through the very young shoot, provided the preparation is thin and examined with a high power of the microscope, the young vascular bundles are found to present a definite and symmetrical structure, easily distinguished from that of the fundamental cell-tissue in which they are, so to speak, embedded (fig. 12).

The cells of the medullary rays are seen in one, two, or several rows, each cell having the form of a parallelopiped or ordinary brick—the bricks being supposed standing on their narrow sides and with the long axes directed radially. The walls in contact with the vascular bundles are thickened, and soon become woody and beset with simple pits; the cells contain protoplasm and nuclei, and in winter become filled to crowding with starch grains. They also contain tannin.

The young vascular bundles, in section, project into the pith—like wedges with a rounded point—giving to the latter the five-rayed shape on the transverse section already referred to (fig. 9).

The cells of the pith also have their walls thickened and pitted, and also contain protoplasm, nuclei, and tannin, and starch in winter. At the rounded angles of the vascular wedges the cells are smaller than elsewhere in the pith, but otherwise their shape, &c., are similar; all the pith-cells are vertically twice or three times as long as broad. Thus the shape of the cells is that of short, polygonal prisms, standing on end and closely packed.

Embedded, as it were, in the smaller pith-cells at the rounded angles of the vascular wedges are the oldest—*i.e.* first-formed—vessels, looking like small holes with very firm outlines (fig. 12, *r*). These are the tracheæ, or vessels with unrollable spiral thickenings on their walls. From their shape and peculiarities they are called spiral vessels, and from their position and development they constitute the first-formed elements of the xylem or wood. They are of very narrow calibre, and stand in radial, short rows, single or branched; those first developed—*i.e.* nearest the pith—are the narrowest, their diameter being often even less than that of the smallest pith-cells among which they lie. As we pass radially out towards the cortex these vessels get wider and wider, but the true spiral vessels are always very narrow (fig. 16, *sp*). Occasionally some of these vessels have annular instead of spiral thickenings.

Of course, their true characters are not elucidated until we compare longitudinal sections of the stem. It is then seen that the spiral thickenings are very closely wound, sometimes to the right, sometimes to the left, and occasionally double. Comparative studies of longitudinal sections also show that these vessels at first simply consist of longitudinal rows of very narrow, vertically placed, cylindrical cells, standing end to end; it is because the adjacent ends become resorbed and disappear that the rows of cells at length form long continuous tubes—vessels, or tracheæ.

Turning once more to the transverse section, as the eye follows the bundle radially outwards the lumina of the vessels in the radial rows are found to become wider and wider, until we meet with vessels with diameters many times greater than that of the pith-cells. The walls of these wider vessels, however, are not strengthened with spiral thickenings, but are thickened and furnished with bordered pits, the shape and characters of which are best seen from the illustrations (figs. 14–16). These larger vessels are not always associated with the radial rows of spiral vessels, but may be scattered between them.

The vessels intermediate between the spiral and the pitted ones are thickened sometimes with reticulations. All these larger vessels have septa inclined towards the medullary rays, and perforated with several long, oval, parallel, horizontal holes: hence the segments are easily macerated and distinguished, and their lengths are found to be variable (fig. 16, *p.v*).

The large pitted vessels form groups with parenchyma and wood-cells scattered between, and are confined chiefly to the inner parts, forming radiating series side by side; in the outer parts of the bundle are

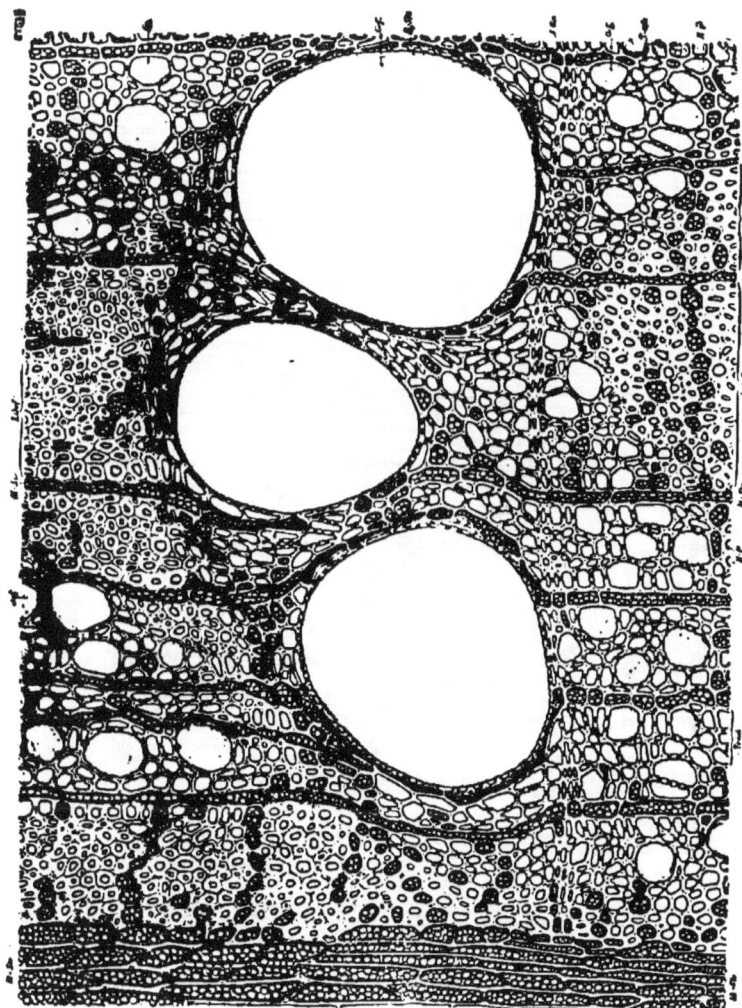

FIG. 13.—Highly-magnified transverse section of wood of oak, showing three of the large pitted vessels (*Gef.*) and a number of smaller ones. *M.Str*, medullary rays, of which part of a large one is shown to the left ; *Librf*, wood-fibres ; *H.P*, wood-parenchyma ; *Trach*, tracheids ; *J.Gr*, boundary of annual ring. (Kny.)

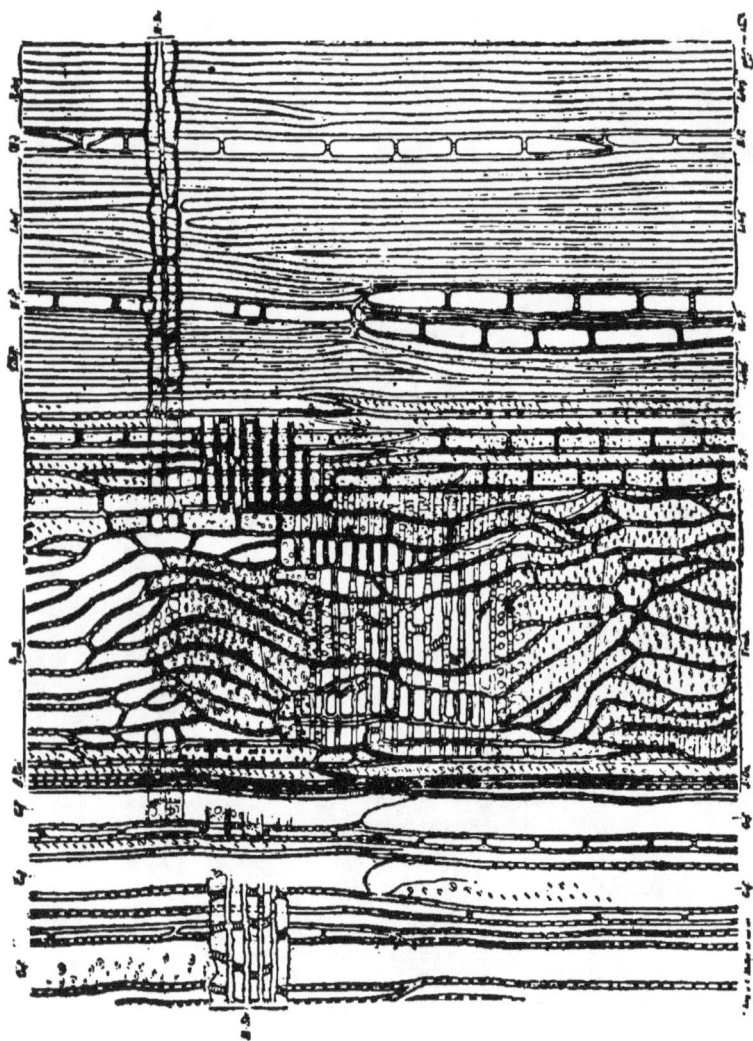

FIG. 14.—Radial longitudinal section of wood of oak (highly magnified). *M.Str*, medullary rays; *Trach*, tracheids; *Gef* (to the left), smaller pitted vessels; *H.P*, wood-fibres; *Librf*, wood-parenchyma. The large mass of tracheids to the left of the centre of the figure lies over one of the broad pitted vessels. *J.Gr*, boundary of annual ring. (Kny.)

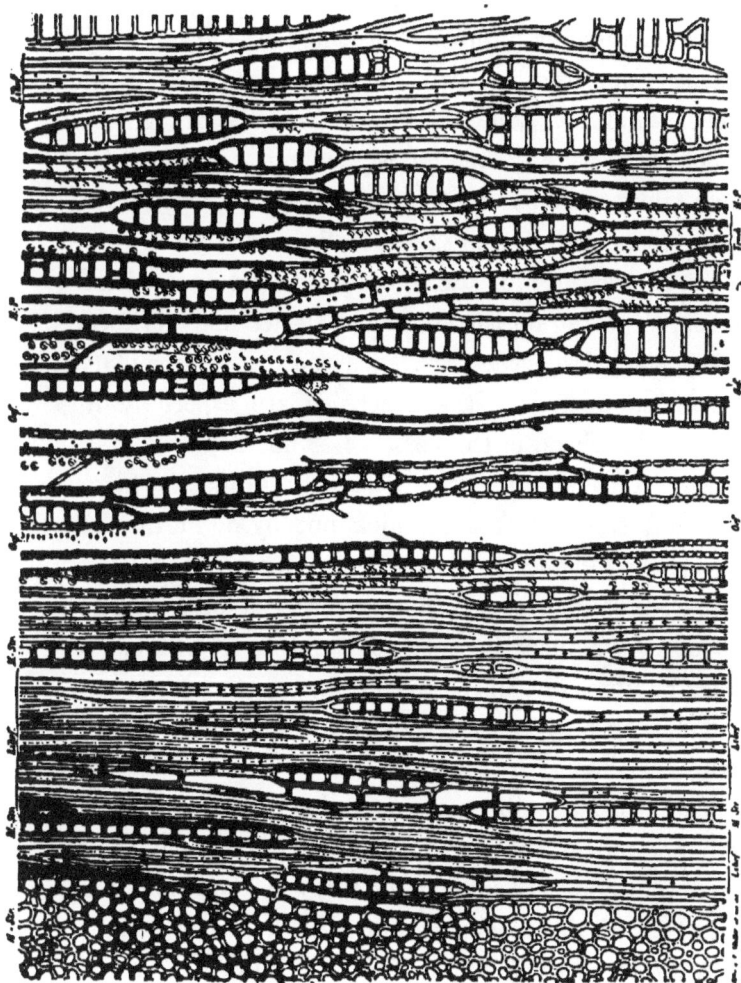

FIG. 15.—Tangential longitudinal section of wood of oak (highly magnified). To the left is a large medullary ray (*M.Sr*), and numerous small ones are seen in various parts of the section—of course, in transverse section. *Librf*, wood-fibres: *Gef*, smaller pitted vessels; *Trach*, tracheids; *H.P*, wood-parenchyma. (Kny.)

various groups of smaller vessels—the groups being rounded, or in radial rows, or curved or oblique rows.

Successive sections prove that the vessels in the bundle change in number—*i.e.* there are fewer when passing from stem to leaf. A vessel may end in an interpectinating, pointed, terminal cell; or it may branch, as it were, dichotomously, owing to fusions with other similar elements; or such a fusion may occur lower down, the original vessel ending blindly.

In the vicinity of the reticulated and first pitted vessels, following on the spiral vessels, we find libriform fibres, tracheids, wood parenchyma, and secondary rays of parenchyma; the tracheids are especially in the neighbourhood of the vessels (*see* fig. 14).

The tracheids are long cells with gradually taper ends, and the walls rather thick but by no means obscuring the lumen; on the walls are numerous, usually elongated, oblique or horizontal bordered pits. These pits occur whether the next element is a tracheid, a vessel, or fibres or cells of any kind (fig. 16, *tr*).

The length of the tracheids varies, and the diameter is also variable.

The libriform fibres are also long cells, but often more pointed at the ends, and their very thick walls almost obliterate the lumen (fig. 16, *f*); their length is about that of the tracheids, but slit-like, small, simple pits are rare on their walls. In the wood of later years, however, the lengths may be different.

There are also elements which stand midway between

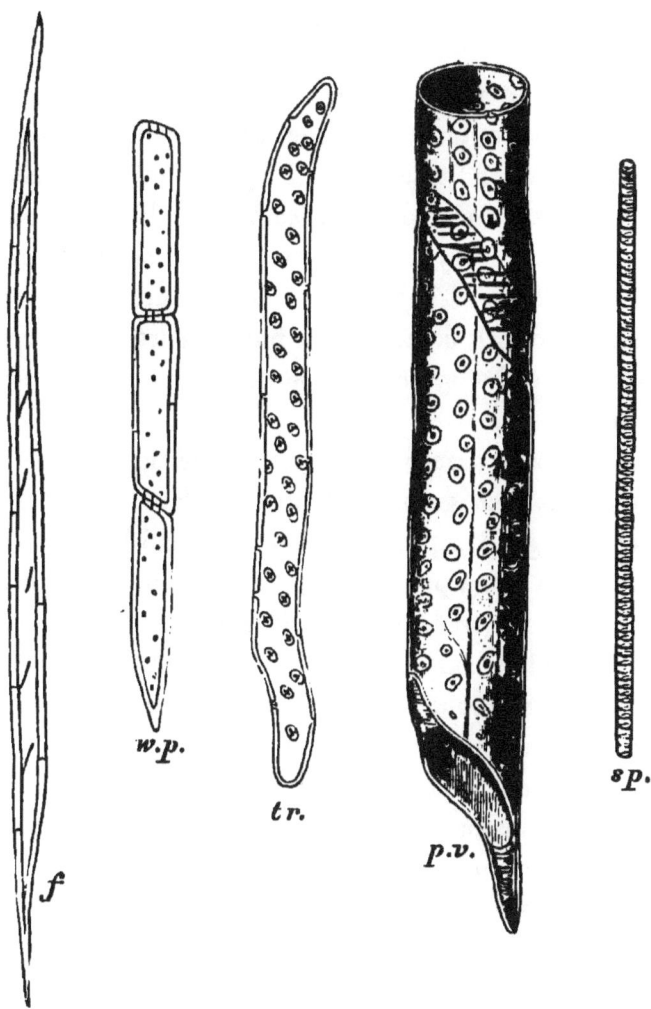

FIG. 16.—The various chief elements of the wood of the oak, isolated by maceration, and highly magnified. *f*, a fibre, distinguished by its thick walls, simple slit-like pits, and no contents; *w.p*, part of a row of wood-parenchyma cells, with simple pits, and containing starch in winter; *tr*, a tracheid, distinguished from the fibre especially by its bordered pits; *p.v*, part of a rather large pitted vessel, made up of communicating segments, each of which corresponds to a tracheid, and has bordered pits on its walls; *sp*, part of a spiral vessel.

the true fibres and tracheids; they occur in those parts
where masses of true fibres abut on the groups consisting of vessels and tracheids.   They resemble tracheids,
but have very few and small, scarcely bordered, oblique,
slit-like pits: every stage can be detected between these
and true fibres.   They must be looked upon as, so to
speak, abnormal, because their numbers are small compared with the typical elements among which they
occur.

The wood-parenchyma consists of vertical groups of
short cells, each group having the fusiform shape of a
tracheid (fig. 16, *w.p*) : hence the upper and lower cell of
each group has a pointed end.   Each group obviously
arises from the transverse divisions of a long, prismatic
cell, pointed at both ends—a cambium cell.   The transverse section is round, and somewhat larger than that of
a tracheid, and the walls are somewhat thinner.   Where
they abut on vessels and tracheids their walls have
bordered pits, but where they stand in contact with
similar groups, or with parenchyma rays, the pits are
simple.   During periods of rest they are loaded with
starch grains.

The length of the groups—*i.e.* of the fusiform cells
cut up into short cells—varies; the shorter ones have
only one transverse division.

The wood-parenchyma is less abundant than the
tracheids and fibres, and predominates in the more
vascular parts; after two to four or more fibres in a
radial row a single parenchyma cell may often be seen,

but other arrangements occur. In the parts where fewer vessels occur it is not uncommon to find a series of radial rows of about six to ten fibres end in a single parenchyma cell, and thus are formed short, tangential rows of wood-parenchyma cells, intercalated, as it were, between the radial rows of other elements (fig. 12, *p*). It often happens, moreover, that reticulated and pitted vessels are closely surrounded by wood-parenchyma.

The secondary medullary rays exist as single radial rows of cells, agreeing in form, &c., with the cells of the primary medullary rays. In contact with one another or with wood parenchyma their walls have simple pits, but they have bordered pits where they abut on tracheids or vessels. In winter these cells are filled with starch. On tangential sections (fig. 15) it is easy to see how the vertical groups of cells have the same origin as the groups of wood-parenchyma cells—the difference being that the cambial cells which are going to be transformed by horizontal divisions, &c., into vertical rows of ray parenchyma, undergo repeated tangential longitudinal divisions, and so continued radial rows are formed. The cells of these rays are often much shorter than those of the wood-parenchyma, yet all gradations occur. The mother-cells may be very long, evidently corresponding to two, and they may also divide in the radial longitudinal plane, and the ray become biseriate.

These secondary rays start (on the transverse section) from the first large vessels, or from younger ones, or they may start from other points. The ray may some-

times cease within the first year's bundle; but the difficulty comes in of deciding whether a continuation occurs
at a higher or lower level.

The cells of the cambium, seen in transverse section,
are rectangular in shape and arranged in regular radial
rows, owing to the regular tangential divisions (fig. 12,
n, m). In longitudinal sections they are found to be like
the tracheids in shape and size, so that they stand one
behind the other at the same level. Regarding the
tangential series in rings, however, they are less regular,
because the tangential longitudinal divisions of two cells
side by side do not lie in the same tangential plane.
This regular radial arrangement would be found in the
xylem also, and is so to a certain extent, but it is disturbed by the differences in diameter which the various
elements attain later. The fibres are most apt to pre-
serve the regularity, but in many cases growth in
length, and the intercalation of oblique septa, disturb it.

In later years the length of the cambial cells increases, and hence the length of the elements in the
wood.

The phloëm or bast of the individual bundle is separated from its neighbours by large rays of parenchyma,
the cells of which agree with the secondary bast-parenchyma rays. As these pass into the cortex they widen,
as they do at the pith (fig. 12).

The oldest portion of the phloëm—that next the
cortex—consists of a group of thick-walled bast fibres
with their lumina nearly obliterated; these are long,

spindle-shaped fibres much like the fibres of the wood.

As a rule, the outer and inner side of these bast groups are in contact with vertical rows of nearly cubical parenchyma cells, strongly thickened on the side next the bast, and each nearly filled with a crystalline clump or with an imperfectly formed crystal of oxalate of lime.   Similar vertical rows of crystal cells may also occur within the groups of bast fibres, the walls of the cubical cells being more or less thickened and simply pitted.   Occasionally a cell here and there retains thin walls.   The vertical rows result from cross-divisions of prosenchymatous mother-cells, the conical ends being found in macerations.

Within the groups of bast fibres are yet other rows, similarly formed, of parenchyma (fig. 17, *bp*), the cells of which are longer, however, attaining the length of the wood-parenchyma; like the latter also their walls are lignified and rather thick, and they contain starch in the winter.   Thus we have parenchyma in the bast. Transitions between these two forms of parenchyma cells are also found.

The cells of the rays between the bast fibres are thickened and pitted; they are rounded, and not in vertical series as in the rest of the rays, but are scattered in no particular order.   Sometimes they are few, and one or all with very thick walls perforated by pit-canals (fig. 17, *bs*).

The remaining younger part of the bast consists

F

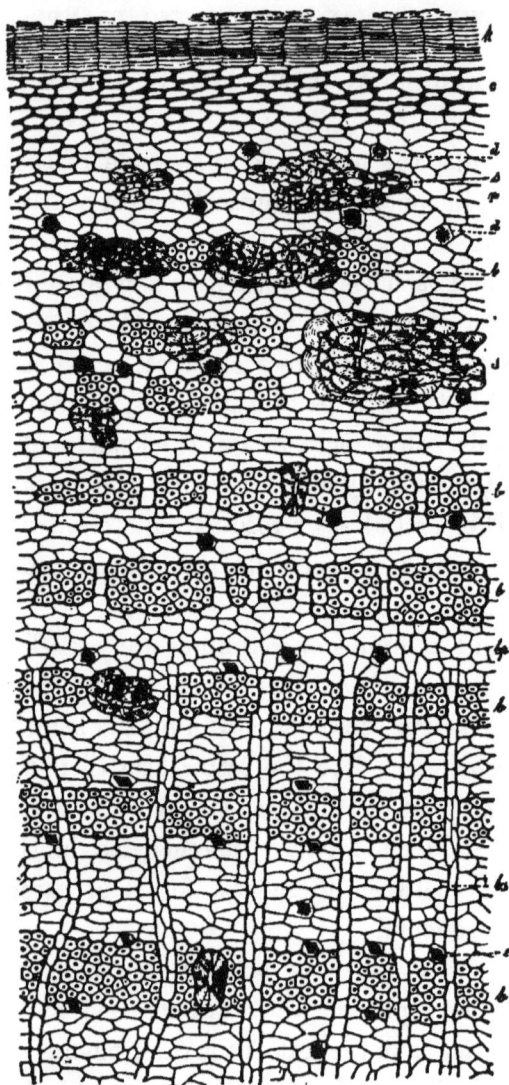

FIG. 17.—Transverse section of cortex and phloëm of oak (highly
magnified). *k*, the periderm (cork), which has replaced the epidermis; *c*, collenchyma; *d*, cells of cortex containing crystals of
oxalate of lime; *s*, schlerenchyma cells. All these belong to the
cortex proper. Below these come the phloëm: *b, b*, groups of hard
bast fibres; *bp*, phloëm-parenchyma; *bs*, medullary ray; *e*, cells
containing crystals of oxalate of lime. (Luerssen.)

chiefly of delicate, apparently irregular parenchyma cells with cellulose walls; this is easily traced to the cambium. The radial rows of the latter can be followed for some distance, the radial diameter of the cells increasing, the walls thickening, and the rectangular shape changing. Displacements from the radial arrangement then occur. A few cells assume a nearly circular form (*i.e.* in transverse section), and the larger ones are effective in causing displacements. The bast-cells developed earlier, and therefore more distant from the cambium zone, now lie in the perceptibly larger periphery, and thus undergo tangential extension or radial compression, and so undergo changes of form. Besides these alterations in form and position, the more delicate bast elements increase in numbers by the development of perpendicular division walls; this is quite clear in those parts nearest the cambium, but further out, where great irregularity occurs, it is impossible to say which cells have arisen direct from the cambium and which by these later divisions. Still, certain thin septa betray their late origin.

On tangential sections we see elongated, pointed, interpectinating cells, with secondary rays of parenchyma between, showing that these are formed and continued by the cambium. Each pointed cell has proceeded from a cambium cell, and indeed only differs in its thicker walls and pits. These cells are still simple, or here and there have a transverse septum obliquely across. If the tangential section is in a slightly older portion, most of the above cells are found to be septate and cut up into parenchyma-like cells—irregular bast-parenchyma. The walls, especially the longitudinal walls, are marked either with crowded small pits, giving a reticulate appearance, or have sieve-plates ; all intermediate stages occur also. The transverse walls are also pitted with sieve-plates.

All the cells of the soft bast contain tannin, and small grains which turn brown in iodine (leucoplasts ?). Very little starch is found in them except in winter. Crystals occur in pitted cells here and there (fig. 18, d and e).

Even in the first year the cambium may produce small groups of thick-walled bast fibres of exactly the same character as those of the primordial groups.

It is obvious that while the wood elements remain fixed in the cylindrical surface where they are developed, the bast elements formed outside the cambium, being driven outwards in consequence of growth in thickness, come to lie in a layer of continually increasing radius. If these bast elements were unyielding and lignified there would be a solid sheath of elements which refused to extend by mechanical distension, cell division, or growth of cell-walls; this would finally rupture under the pressure from within. This is prevented by the division and growth of the chief phloëm elements.

In the vascular-bundle system of the stem there are no essential differences in structure as we pass from one region to another; the only variations are in the thickness or breadth of the bundles at different points, such as where other bundles join or leave them.   As the

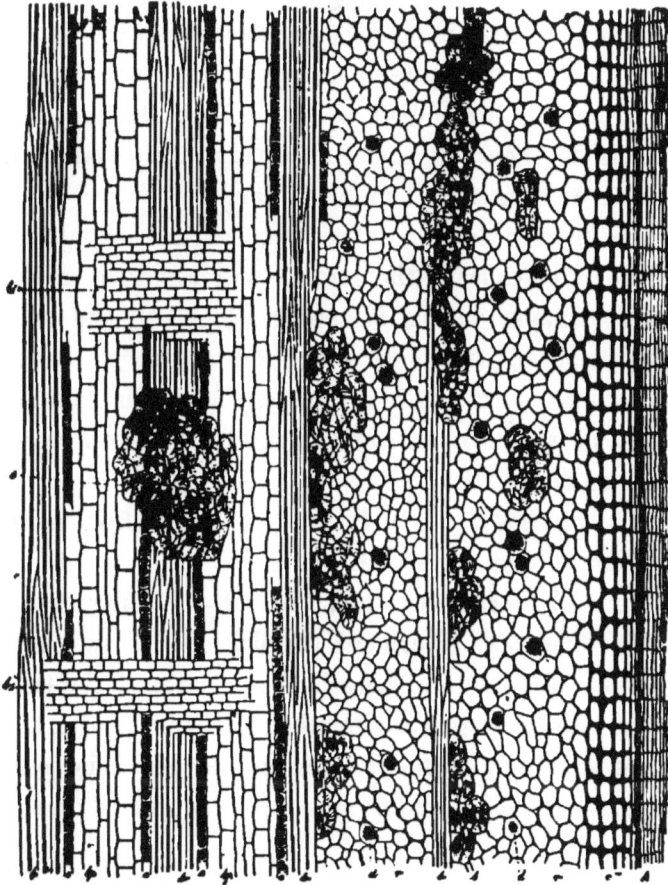

FIG. 18.—Longitudinal radial section of the cortex and phloëm of oak.   References as in fig. 17.   (Luerssen.)

leaf-trace passes into the venation of the leaf the ends become thinner (fig. 21), and the same is found as it tails

off below ; changes in structure also appear in the
leaves.

The first noticeable change is the diminution in the
number of wood fibres and the presence of narrow vessels
only.   As the trace passes through the cortex to the leaf
the actual number of both xylem- and phloëm-elements
diminishes; hence it comes about that the bundles in
the leaves consist to a relatively large extent of spiral
vessels in the xylem and of sieve-tubes in the phloëm.
As the bundles leave the midrib and larger veins the
true continuous vessels disappear altogether, and only
spindle-shaped tracheids with reticulated or spiral
thickenings occur, fitting obliquely at their pointed
ends, and which are shorter and shorter as we approach
the ends of the bundles.

The phloëm also is at length reduced to little more
than one or two sieve-tubes, the segments of which are
shorter and shorter as we near the end.   The shortening
of the elements is in evident correlation with the early
cessation of growth in length of the parts of the leaf,
and the diminution of the number of elements with the
decreased supply of fluids, &c., on the one hand, and
the smaller weight and strains to be supported on the
other.

We may sum up the changes in structure towards
the ends of the vascular bundles thus.   The thickening
of the walls is less, and the elements become narrower
and shorter ; the xylem becomes simplified by the loss
of fibres and vessels, until finally only delicate tracheids

are left (fig. 21), the thickenings of which are at length
not spirals or nets for the most part, but irregular pittings.
Moreover, they are nearly isolated.   Nevertheless, the
inner elements can be distinguished as primary tracheal
elements, because, being earlier formed, they partook
more in what elongation occurred, and their spirals, for
instance, are wider apart.

In the midrib, in proportion as the structural changes
go on, the bundles approach one another, the separating
parenchyma becoming narrower and narrower.   The
pith consists of parenchyma, chiefly unlignified and
with simple pits, but as the bundles are approached
the cells become longer and lignified; the rays between
the xylem groups are also lignified.

Towards autumn the cells of the pith and rays fill
with starch; this is nearly, but not quite, all resorbed
before the leaf falls.

The termination of the bundles in the leaf consists
only of a few narrow spiral and reticulated cells, which
at last become very short and variable in shape, and of
a few small sieve elements and cells (*see* Chapter VI.).

CHAPTER VI

THE SEEDLING AND YOUNG PLANT (*continued*)

THE BUDS AND LEAVES

THE. buds of the oak—those in the leaf-axils as well as
those at the tips of the young shoots—are characteris-
tically short and broad ovoid bodies, consisting of numerous overlapping brown scales covered with short, silky
hairs, especially at the margins (fig. 19). These scales are
really the stipules of arrested leaves, as is shown by the
proper leaf-blades being developed as well under certain
circumstances, such as when nutritive materials are
directed to the young buds. The same morphological
fact is also shown by the position of the inflorescences
and young leaves higher up in the bud, for they spring
from between the scales, and not from their axils proper
(*see* fig. 32). It is of the highest importance to understand
that a bud is simply the young state of a shoot, and that
it consists of the growing-point of the shoot enveloped
by closely-folded leaf structures. In the oak the buds
are already formed before the end of June, and on
looking closely into the axils of the leaves on the

young shoots—which have by that time ceased to
elongate to any considerable extent further—they may
be seen as small, green, hairy bodies. During the remainder of the summer the chief changes going on in

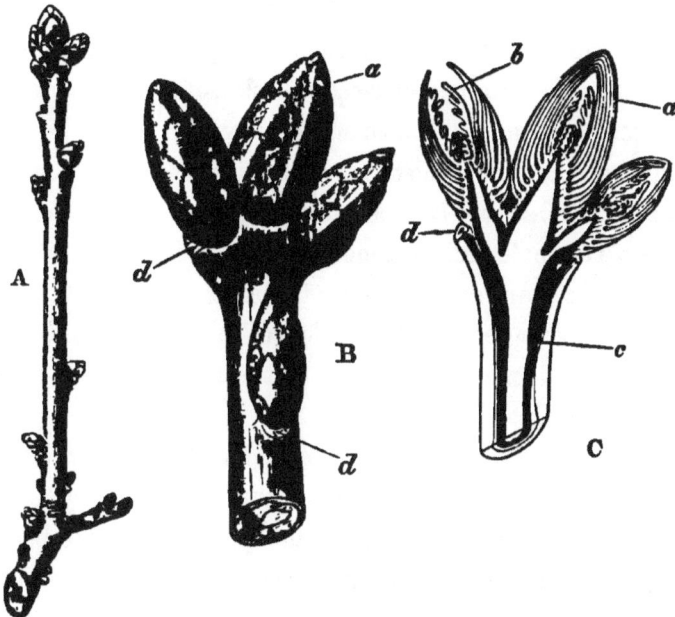

FIG. 19.—A. End of a branch of oak showing the characteristic winter buds. B. A group of buds (slightly magnified); a, bud-scales; d, leaf-scars. C. The same, in
longitudinal section : a, bud-scales (stipules); b, young
leaves; c, vascular bundles; d, leaf-scars. (Prantl and
Hartig.)

these buds is a slow swelling, due to the gradual storing
up of nutritive materials in the pith and growing-point
and to the slow division of the cells.

A vertical section through the bud at the end of the
autumn shows the following structures (fig. 19, c). A

conical growing-point, consisting of embryonic tissue,
occupies the centre; around this, arranged in a close
spiral, are several young rudiments of foliage leaves, each
consisting of meristem, the cells of which are undergoing
divisions. The youngest leaf is next the apex of the cone
—*i.e.* the order of development is acropetal—and each is
folded with the upper surfaces of each half in contact; two
extremely minute stipules accompany each leaf. Lower
down on the cone come the numerous (about thirty) overlapping scales, and between several pairs of the upper of
these the male inflorescences develop. The female inflorescences are developed in the axils of two or three
of the above-described true leaves in a terminal bud;
they are not normally formed in the lateral buds of the
shoot (*see* Chapter IX.).

All the leaves of the shoot may have such buds
formed in their axils during the summer, but only some
of them develop in the following spring; it is the buds
in the axils of the lower leaves of the shoot which
usually come to nothing.

The normal course of events is that the bud-scales
(stipules) become dry, and the protected growing-point,
with its rudimentary leaves and flowers, passes into a
dormant condition lasting through the winter; but it is
a very common event, especially in a wet autumn following a dry, hot summer, to find the winter buds beginning to shoot out in August, and not passing into the
prolonged state of dormancy. Such shoots are known
as Lammas shoots. In some districts the oak forms

numbers of these Lammas shoots every year, and the tendency to produce them seems to be capable of being inherited.

The process of sprouting, or putting forth the shoot from the bud, is the same in all the cases. As the temperature and other conditions improve in the spring, for instance, the process of cell-division in the growing-point (and its derivatives, the young leaves, &c.) goes on rapidly, and the stores of nourishment already there and in the pith and other tissues close at hand are used up. This originates a series of currents of food materials set-ting slowly towards these centres of consumption from other parts of the tree, and very soon the numerous cells developed begin to absorb water with relatively enor-mous rapidity and vigour. This brings about two chief changes—the rapid elongation of the parts of the cone situated between the points of insertion of successive leaves (*i.e.* the internodes), and the almost simultaneous expan-sion of the hitherto small and folded leaves. Thus the rapid extension of the shoot is due almost entirely to the energetic absorption of water into cells for the most part already in existence. The chief changes which follow consist in the perfection of the structures—the develop-ment and thickening of vascular tissues, cell-walls, &c.

This process of rapid extension does not occur in the internodes between the bud-scales, or, at any rate, to a slight degree only, just sufficient to enable the shoot to throw the scales off; hence the base of the outgrown shoot shows a number of small scars in a close spiral.

These scars of the stipular bud-scales, like those of fallen leaves, exhibit the points of rupture of the vascular bundles which ran across from the bundles of the bud-axis.   It only remains to point out that the buds vary in size and vigour according to the age and condition of the tree; the buds on oaks less than fifty years old very rarely have inflorescences developed in them, and I shall defer the consideration of these till we come to the flower.

The mature leaf of the oak (fig. 20) is obovate in general outline, with rather deep sinuses cutting the margin on each side into about six or eight rounded lobes; the apex is rounded or blunt, and some variation occurs in the degree of incision between the lobes.   The base either tapers slightly into an evident petiole, or it is prolonged on either side of a very short petiole so as to form small auricles.   In the commonest variety the margins and surfaces of the leaf are quite smooth, but the race-form known as *Quercus sessiliflora* has the young leaves pubescent beneath.

The venation consists of a midrib running from base to apex, and pinnate lateral ribs running from the midrib at an angle of about 45° to the tip of each lobe, the points of origin being alternate or nearly opposite, and the angle referred to subtending forwards.   These principal ribs are prominent below but not at all so above.   The leaf-tissue (mesophyll) between these is permeated by numerous smaller vascular bundles united into an irregular network, but so arranged that

they leave between them nearly equal small areas not
traversed by bundles.

FIG. 20.—Sprigs of oak, showing the habit and the arrangement of the acorns, &c., in September. (After Kotschy.)

When young the leaves are red, gradually becoming
a bright apple-green, and finally—in the autumn—

becoming russet-brown in colour. Young oaks retain
their dead leaves till far into the winter, and even old
trees usually have some leaves attached till January.
The young leaves secrete small quantities of sweet
liquid on the superior face of the lamina, and are much
visited by bees and wasps; this honey must come
through the membrane. As the leaves
approach maturity the lamina becomes
bright and hard.

The arrangement of the leaves is expressed by the fraction $\frac{2}{5}$, as already described, each node giving off one leaf at an open angle, the points of insertion being so arranged that a line drawn from the insertion of a given lower leaf,

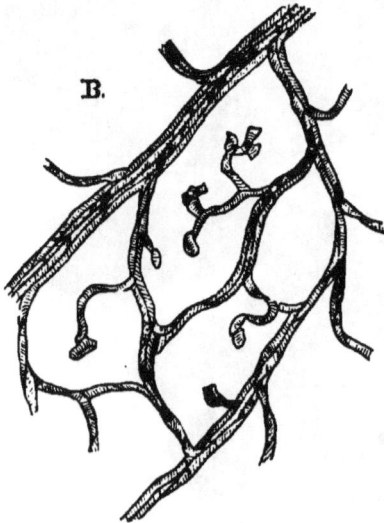

Fig. 21.—A portion of the ultimate
ramifications of the vascular bundles,
showing tracheids only, isolated from
the leaf by maceration.

and joining it to the
points of insertion of those above, passes twice round the
twig before we arrive at the leaf situated vertically above
the one started from, and this upper leaf is the sixth
above. Although this is the commonest and normal
arrangement, however, other dispositions are occasionally

met with on the same plant. The young leaves are folded in the bud in such a manner that the two halves of the lamina lie one on the other, the upper surfaces being in contact (conduplicate vernation), the margins being therefore turned upwards.

In order to understand the structure of the leaf, let us look at a section cut neatly across the midrib and lamina, and examined with the microscope. It is found to consist of three principal parts—an epidermis above and below, and all round the margins, and therefore over the whole of the leaf; this epidermis is, in fact, a continuation of that of the young shoot-axis, and envelops the whole of the remaining leaf-tissues. Inside this we have the main mass of the leaf substance —called the *mesophyll*—consisting of thin-walled cells arranged in a peculiar manner, and containing (in addition to less obvious structures) large numbers of green chlorophyll corpuscles; it is the predominance of these corpuscles which causes the leaves to appear uniformly green. Here and there we see vascular bundles, embedded, as it were, in the mesophyll, cut across in various directions, and when it is remembered that these vascular bundles constitute the venation of the leaf this phenomenon is easily explained.

As we have already seen, the vascular bundles of the venation (fig. 20) are simply the much-branched and thinned-off upper ends of the vascular bundles from the shoot-axis, the lower ends of which join the vascular system of the latter lower down. Now the next point to be

clearly apprehended is that these vascular bundles of the
leaves have the double duty of supporting the flattened

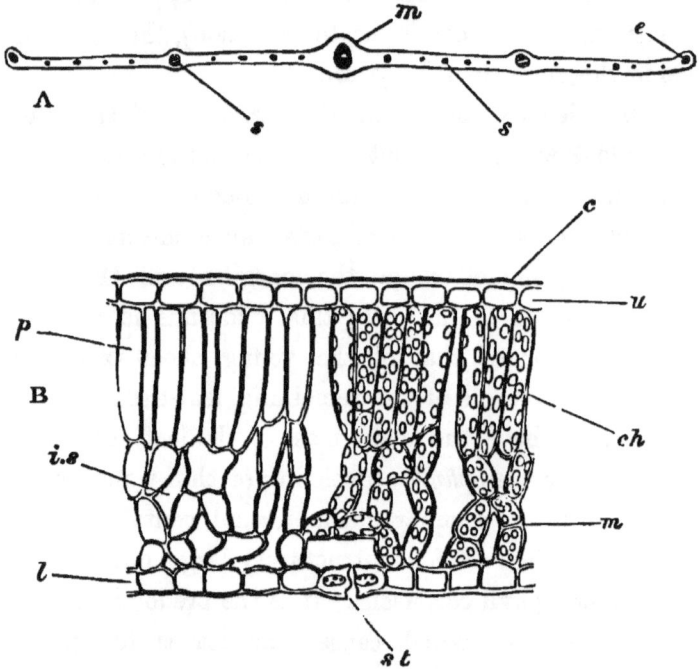

FIG. 22.—Sections across the leaf of oak. A. Slightly magnified and semi-diagrammatic, to show the general
arrangement of the principal vascular bundles as seen
cut across; *m*, midrib; *c*, marginal veins; *s*, lateral
branches of midrib.   Other smaller veins scattered between.   B. A highly magnified vertical section of part
of the above at a place free from vascular bundles:
u, upper epidermis, with cuticle, *c*; *p*, palisade cells; *ch*,
chlorophyll corpuscles, only drawn in a few cells; *m*,
spongy tissue of mesophyll; *i.s*, intercellular passages
communicating with the stoma, *st*, in the lower epidermis, *l*.

mass of leaf-tissue, and of carrying to and from its cells
the water from the roots and the organic substances

formed in the cells of the leaves. The water, with salts in solution, coming from the soil, after it has been absorbed by the root-hairs, passes up the wood (xylem) of the roots and stem, through the vessels of the petioles and leaf-venation, and is finally distributed to the cells of the mesophyll; the substances formed in these cells then pass down by the phloëm (sieve-tubes, &c.) of the venation and leaf-stalk, and thence are distributed to other parts of the plant.

Now let us look at the mesophyll which these vascular bundles support and serve as conduits for. It consists of two distinct parts (fig. 22). Beneath the upper epidermis, the cells of which are fitted closely together without intercellular spaces and are devoid of chlorophyll corpuscles, there are one or two rows of vertical sausage-shaped cells, closely arranged like the wooden railings of a complete palisade—consequently they are termed the palisade cells. The lower moiety of the mesophyll, on the other hand, is composed of irregular cells with large intercellular spaces between them, and this loose, spongy tissue, as it is aptly called, abuts below on the lower epidermis. Both the palisade cells and those of the spongy tissue contain numerous chlorophyll corpuscles, as said.

This lower epidermis is worth a few minutes' consideration. It, like the upper epidermis, is also composed chiefly of closely fitting cells devoid of chlorophyll corpuscles, excepting that here and there we notice pairs of smaller cells containing chlorophyll—each pair with a

G

minute gap between them, and the gap communicates
with the intercellular air-cavities between the cells of
the spongy mesophyll (fig. 22, *st*). If we remove a piece
of this epidermis, and look at it as laid flat (instead of in
section) under the microscope, we find that these pairs
of small cells are shaped somewhat like a small mouth,
the two curved lips of which are formed by the two cells
just mentioned, and the orifice of which is the gap just
referred to (fig. 23). These two lips are called the guard-
cells, and the whole apparatus is termed a *stoma*.   It is
necessary to realise two great facts about these stomata
on the under surface of the leaf: firstly, there are several
hundreds of thousands of them on an oak-leaf, each
square millimetre having from 300 to 350 of them
scattered over it ; and, secondly, each one can open or
close its little aperture by the approximation or divarica-
tion of the inner concave sides of the curved guard-cells.

   If this is clear it will be readily understood that
these stomata can regulate the amount of water passing
off by evaporation from the walls of the millions of
cells of the mesophyll, especially if the further fact is
borne in mind that water-vapour scarcely passes at all
through the close-fitting epidermis cells themselves.

   We are now in a position to form a sort of picture
of the mechanism of the shoot and root in regard to this
matter. The root-hairs absorb water from the soil, and
in this water there are dissolved small quantities of the
soluble salts of the earth—chiefly sulphates, nitrates,
and phosphates of lime, magnesia, and potash—just as

there are in ordinary well-water. This extremely
dilute solution passes into the root-fibres and up

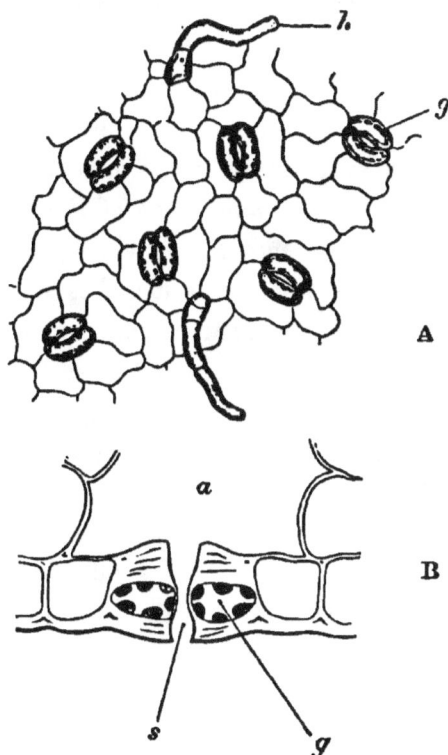

FIG. 23.—A. A small piece of the lower epidermis removed
(and highly magnified) to show the stomata, *g* ; *h*, minute
hairs. The guard-cells contain chlorophyll corpuscles,
whereas the ordinary epidermal cells do not. B. A stoma
in vertical median section, cut across its longer axis ; *a*,
intercellular space ; *g*, guard-cell with chlorophyll corpuscles ; *s*, orifice of stoma.

through the vessels, &c., of the vascular bundles of the
roots, collecting into the larger and larger channels
until it reaches the stem ; here it passes up the xylem

to the branches, petioles, and leaf-venation—always in the wood—and is finally distributed to the mesophyll cells, which absorb it and evaporate the greater part of the water into the intercellular passages communicating with the outer air through the stomata.

Two points need notice here. The first is that this absorption and evaporation in the mesophyll constitute a cause of the upward movement of the water in the vascular bundles—a movement which is propagated through the whole stem until it makes itself effective even in the roots. The exact mechanism of the move-ment in the stem itself is too complex for discussion here; but I may sum up the matter by saying that the disappearance of the water at the surfaces of the leaves starts a series of flows in directions of least resistance towards the mesophyll, and as long as the evaporation goes on more water flows into the cells, to replace that lost, from the vessels of the stem, when the water-columns are supported and moved partly by capillarity and by the air bubbles in the cavities, and partly by a peculiar co-operation of the living cells of the medullary rays. The second point referred to above is that the evaporation from the mesophyll cells will be the more rapid in proportion as the air outside is drier and the stomata wide open; and the more energetic this evaporation is, the more salts the mesophyll cells will acquire in a given time, because, of course, the salts do not pass away in the evaporated water but are left in the cells. It has been calculated that an oak-tree may have 700,000 leaves, and that 111,225 kilogrammes of water may pass off from its surface in the five months from June to October, and that 226 times its own weight of water may pass through it in a year.

Now comes the question—What are the salts needed for that so much mechanism should be expended on their accumulation? To answer this we must look at the mesophyll cells a little more closely.

Each of these consists of a thin cellulose cell-wall, lined with colourless protoplasm, which encloses a large sap-cavity (vacuole); in the protoplasm are embedded a number of bright green, rounded chlorophyll corpuscles, a relatively large nucleus, and a few less conspicuous granules, &c. The cell-sap contains various substances dissolved in water. Some of these substances are salts and other materials ready to be made use of; others are, so to speak, waste products or worked-up materials that are going to be got rid of, or sent to places where they will be made use of, respectively.

In the colourless protoplasm which lines the interior of the cell-wall and surrounds the cell-sap we find a nucleus and the chlorophyll corpuscles, as said, and a few words must be devoted to the latter. Each chlorophyll corpuscle consists of a rounded mass of protoplasmic substance of somewhat spongy texture, containing the peculiar green body, chlorophyll, embedded in it as in a matrix. These chlorophyll corpuscles are living organs, and they require food materials, water, oxygen, &c., for the support of their life processes, just as do the other living parts of the cell—*e.g.* the colourless proto-plasm and nucleus. They obtain these from the cell-sap, through the agency of the colourless protoplasm in which they reside.

In order that they may perform their functions properly, however, it is essential that they be exposed to light; this is effected by their being in cells which are disposed in thin layers, such as we have seen the mesophyll of the leaf to be. In fact, the flat, thin, expanded form of the leaf is a direct adaptation to the end that these chlorophyll corpuscles shall be properly illuminated by the sunlight; moreover, the large in-tercellular passages which communicate by thousands of stomata with the atmosphere ensure their being thoroughly aërated. In addition to allowing the free access of the oxygen of the air, moreover, these inter-cellular passages admit of the small quantities of carbon dioxide in the atmosphere also reaching the chlorophyll corpuscles. Oxygen and carbon dioxide, therefore, are found dissolved with the other materials in the cell-sap which saturates the protoplasm and reaches the chlorophyll corpuscles.

These facts premised, we are in a position to follow generally the astounding transformations which go on in these millions of chlorophyll corpuscles in the oak-leaf. Carbon dioxide and water exist side by side in the protoplasm of the chlorophyll corpuscle, and rays of sunlight—*i.e.* energetic vibrations of the ether which pervades the universe—penetrate into the system. By means of the energy thus derived from the sun, the molecules of carbon dioxide and water are broken up in the meshes of this chlorophyll corpuscle, and experiments prove that the chlorophyll substance plays the part of the ' trap to catch a sunbeam.' We are not concerned with the hypothetical explanations offered for all the details of this remarkable process, but the present position of science enables us to say that, be these what they may, the chlorophyll corpuscle gains energy form the sun, and brings this energy to bear on the carbon dioxide and water in such a way that it does work in tearing asunder their molecules in the substance of the corpuscle. Then a curious series of results follows. The carbon, oxygen, and hydrogen undergo new rearrangements, which amount finally to this—the substance known as starch, and consisting of carbon, hydrogen, and oxygen, is built up in the form of granules in the chlorophyll corpuscle, and the surplus oxygen escapes into the sap and finds its way to the intercellular passages, and thence through the stomata into the atmosphere.

It will be obvious from the foregoing that the granules of starch represent so much matter (especially carbon) obtained from the atmosphere outside the plant, and so much energy obtained from the sun; each granule may therefore be regarded as a packet of stored energy and matter won from the external universe.

The limits of this little book will not allow of my going into details concerning the use which the plant

makes of this starch, and it must suffice to say that
the starch serves as the basis of all the constructive
materials used by the tree. Thus it is converted into
a soluble form, and combined with nitrogen, phosphorus,
sulphur, &c. (obtained from the earth-salts), to make new
protoplasmic materials, and it passes down from the
leaves to nourish all the living cells that require it, in
the embryonic tissue at the apex of the roots, and that
at the apex of the stem and branches, buds, &c., and some
of it passes to nourish the cambium cells, the developing
flowers, acorns, &c.—in short, wherever new organic material is needed it is supplied from these stores formed
by the green leaves waving in the sunshine. If we
reflect that the little embryo in the acorn starts its life
with only a minute store of starch and proteids in its
cotyledon, and that all the tons of organic material
(chiefly wood) found in an old oak-tree have been super-
added to this by the action of the leaves—the small
proportion of salts taken up by the roots being quite
inconsiderable in comparison—we obtain some idea of
the enormous gain of matter and energy from the outside
universe which goes on each summer.

CHAPTER VII

WE may now suppose the young oak-plant to be rapidly developing into a tree. Technically the seedling is said to be a plant after the first year, and when it reaches the height of a few feet the young tree is called a sapling; these ideas are by no means well defined, however, and we may regard them as arbitrary terms of little or · no scientific value.

The principal changes which are noticeable as the little tree grows larger are the gradual increase in the length and thickness of the stem, and in the number and spread of the branches put forth year after year. Corresponding with these increments, each spring sees a greater number of leaves than the one before, and it is easy to prove that the roots also become more numerous and complex each season.

The above simply expresses certain facts of observation, but it is more accurate to link them together as follows.

In each successive season of growth the young oak develops more leaves than it did before—in other words,

the total area of the leaf-surface exposed to the air and
sunlight is larger each successive summer than it was
the previous one. Several very important consequences
follow from this. In the first place, the larger area of
leaf-surface evaporates more water than before, and as
this water is derived from the soil the absorbing surface
of the roots has to increase, or the larger supplies needed
could not be obtained. In the second place, these larger
and larger quantities of water require corresponding
increase in the sectional area of the pipes or water conduits—*i.e.* the vessels of the wood—through which they
have to pass in order to reach the leaves. This is ensured
by the increase in diameter of the stem and main root
and their chief branches, a larger number of vessels, &c.,
being added each season. In the third place, as the
leaf-crown enlarges its weight increases, and the surface
it exposes to the swaying action of the wind is corre-
spondingly greater; consequently the necessity arises
for more strength and rigidity in the supporting stem,
and for a larger hold on the soil on the part of the root-
system, which has to withstand the lever action of the
swaying tree. These needs, again, are met by the thickening of the woody parts of the shoot-axis and roots, and
by the greater spread and increased number of points of
contact in the soil of the latter.

Correlated with these phenomena we have the increased leaf-surface playing the part of an enlarging
manufactory, which turns out increased supplies of constructive materials each summer; for it is in the leaves

that the substances for making new roots and shoots, new wood, and new leaves, &c., are constructed.   It is in the increased area of this leaf laboratory that the larger supplies of salts, dissolved in the larger quantities of water from the soil, are brought into relations with the increased quantities of carbonaceous substance obtained from the air in the chlorophyll corpuscles, and consequently a larger yield of plant-forming materials is possible to meet the demands of the ever growing organs.

My present purpose is to describe how the thickening process occurs in the older roots, for it is evident at a glance that the strong woody roots of a large tree have undergone many changes since they were the thin filiform rootlets we met with in the young plant (see fig. 7). Not only have they increased in diameter, but they now consist almost entirely of wood, protected by a relatively thin, brown, corky covering, reminding one of certain kinds of bark.

The first changes which take place when the young, thin roots begin to thicken are—first the piliferous layer dies away and the outer cells of the cortex turn brown; then a cylindrical layer of cork is developed in the pericycle, and as this cork is impervious to water it cuts off the cortex from communication with the axis-cylinder, and consequently the cortex gradually shrivels up and is thrown off.

Meanwhile active divisions have been going on in the cells immediately inside the phloëm groups of the axis-cylinder (see fig. 5), and especially by means of tangential walls. The result of this activity is the development of a cambium layer, as it is called, immediately inside the five phloëm groups of the axis-cylinder, and this layer becomes continuous all round the axis-cylinder, but is so arranged that it runs *outside* the primary xylem groups and *inside* the primary phloëm groups (fig. 24, *cam*). This cambium layer is a hollow cylindrical layer of thin-walled cells, full of protoplasm, and somewhat longer than they are broad or deep, and these cells have the peculiarity of dividing very rapidly, especially by tangential walls, so that cell multiplication goes on very rapidly, and the layer would soon become very thick if no other changes occurred. As the new cells are formed, however, those on the outer side of the cylinder—*i.e.* those nearest the phloëm—become for the most part converted into sieve-tubes and cells of the phloëm; while the much more numerous cells formed on the inner side—*i.e.* nearest the centre of the axis-cylinder—are chiefly converted into vessels and cells of the xylem. This xylem and phloëm developed by the cambium are termed secondary xylem and secondary phloëm respectively, and it will be noticed that whereas the secondary phloëm is deposited radially on the inner side of the primary phloëm, the secondary xylem is placed *between* the primary xylem groups, and not radially outside them (fig. 24, *se.x* and *se.ph*). Moreover, the youngest vessels are now nearest the cambium, whence the order of development has become the converse of that of the primary xylem; there are also no spiral vessels formed now. In fact, the structure of the vascular bundles of the root has now changed its character, and from this point forwards the root increases in thickness exactly as the stem does, whence I refer the reader to the following chapter for further details.

The development of the layers of cork which now surround the thickening axis-cylinder go on forming year after year, as the cambium forms more xylem and phloëm and so thickens the root; were this not the case the layer of cork would soon be ruptured as the root increases in diameter. Such rupture, in fact, does occur, but the cork-forming tissue in the pericycle goes on growing and acts as a cork-cambium, and repeatedly develops more cork to make good the layers which are being split and worn off in the soil.

From what has been said it will be understood that a transverse section of an old root differs entirely in structure from that of a young one, although all the changes in the former can be correlated with the primary structures of the latter. In the first place, such a section shows no piliferous layer or cortex, both having been sloughed off long ago; the protective function of these layers is now assumed by the cork jacket (often called periderm) developed by the cork-cambium cylinder in the pericycle, and even this will not show all the cork that the cambium has developed, because many outer layers will have flaked away, just as the present outer layers are doing.

Then, inside this periderm we shall find the phloëm,

forming an almost continuous ring (fig. 24, *se.ph*), and consisting chiefly of the sieve-tubes and cells developed from the cambium cylinder, the small primary phloëm

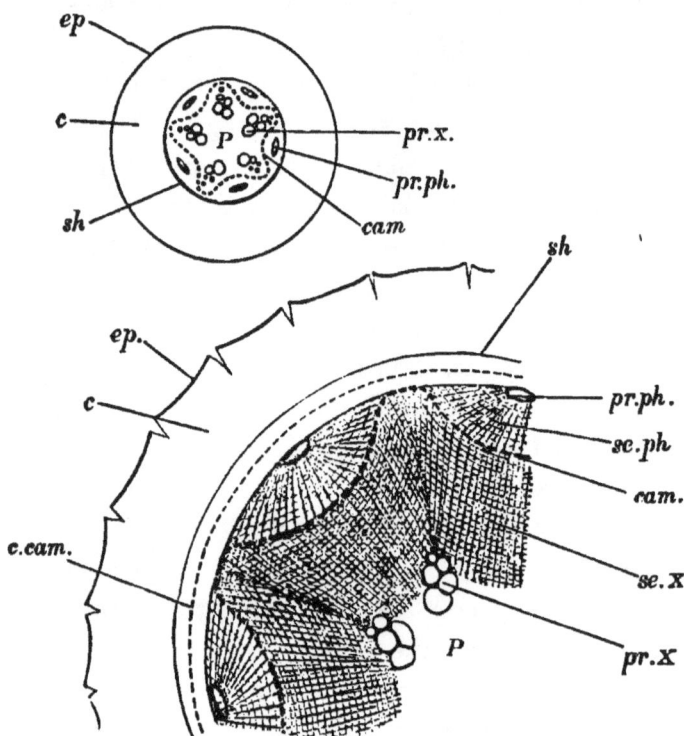

FIG. 24.—Transverse sections (semi-diagrammatic) of roots of oak, to be compared with fig. 7. The smaller figure, above, shows the cambium ring, *cam*, now developed as a continuous layer running inside the primary phloëm, *pr.ph*, and outside the primary xylem, *pr.x*; and the larger figure shows the results of its activity in the formation of secondary phloëm, *se.ph*, inside the primary, and secondary xylem, *se.x*, between the primary xylem groups. In both cases, *ep*, piliferous layer; *c*, cortex; *P*, pith; *sh*, endodermis. Within the latter lies the pericycle, in which the cork cambium, *o.cam*, is now developed.

masses being almost undistinguishably pressed into these (*pr.ph*).

In the centre of the section will be a small speck, around which the microscopic primary xylem groups (*pr.x*) are arranged, but these, again, are merged between the relatively huge masses of secondary xylem which makes up by far the major part of the whole (*se.x*). The thin cambium ring can be distinguished running between the xylem and phloëm as a fine line. Certain concentric annular lines may be seen on the section, and each of these marks the position in which the cambium rested during the winter of some previous year. They are the boundaries of concentric zones, termed annual rings, and the thickness of wood which makes up any one annual ring represents the activity of the cambium during that particular year.

Traversing these annual rings at right angles are fine medullary rays. About five broader ones may be found corresponding to the radii on which the primary xylem groups were formed, but these are not developed by the cambium as the finer ones are. As I shall have to speak of annual rings and secondary medullary rays at greater length when describing the thickening processes in the stem, and as they are formed in the same way in both cases, we may defer their consideration for the present.

Mention must now be made of a remarkable biological phenomenon in connection with the roots of the oak. This is the very common occurrence of young root-

lets clothed by a fungus mycelium; the mycelium is
found as a thin sheet of closely-woven hyphæ continuous
over the whole of the tip, and sending processes in
between the cells of the dermatogen, but not into the

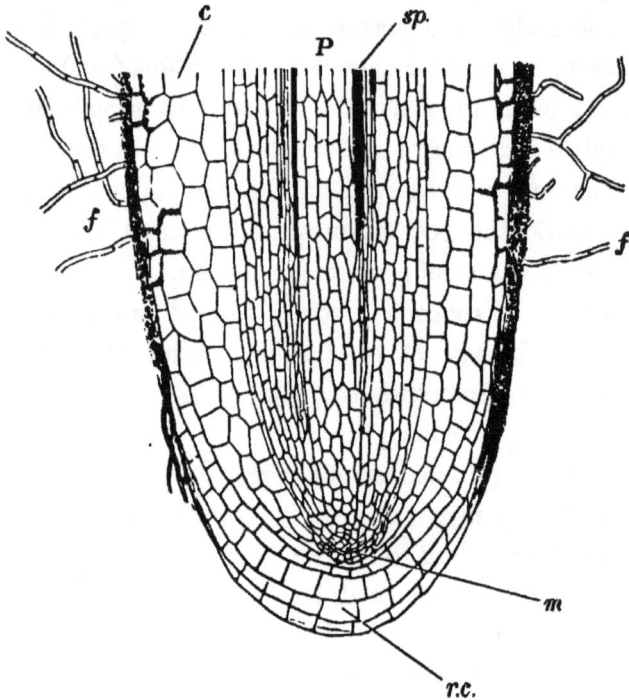

Fig. 25.—Longitudinal section of the tip of one of the
roots marked *m* in fig. 7, the outer layers of which are
infested with fungus hyphæ, *f* (mycorhiza); *r.o*, root-
cap; *m*, embryonic tissue from which all originates; *P*,
pith; *sp*, spiral vessels of the primary xylem; *c*, cortex.

cavities of the cells nor deeper into the tissues. Loose
hyphæ also radiate into the soil around, and often simulate
the root-hairs of other plants, which, in fact, they are

said to replace (fig. 25, f). These hyphæ are extremely fine tubes of a cellulose-like substance, filled with the living protoplasm of the fungus, and possess the remarkable property of being able to bore their way through or between the cellulose walls of the roots. The fungus attacks the plant about the second year, and it is not difficult to find true root-hairs on the young root-system when the apices are still free from the fungus mycelium. The parts of the root attacked alter their form slightly; they grow more slowly in length, and assume a fleshy, coral-like appearance (fig. 7, m). Such a fungus-clothed root is called a *mycorhiza*, and the view is gaining ground that the symbiosis between the fungus and the root is of advantage to the oak. It has even been suggested that the mycelium performs the functions of root-hairs to the root, absorbing water and nutritive materials from the soil and passing them on to the oak, in return for a certain small proportion of organic substance which the latter can well afford. At any rate, it may be that the fungus hurries the decomposition of vegetable remains in such a way that they become available to the roots sooner than would otherwise be the case. The systematic position of these remarkable fungi is not yet ascertained, but there is some evidence for the view that the mycelium is that of a truffle, though the question is still an open one.

CHAPTER VIII

THE TREE—ITS SHOOT-SYSTEM

WHEN we cut into an old branch or stem of the oak
(fig. 26), it is at once obvious that considerable changes
have been produced since it was a twig or young shoot-
axis, such as exists in the young plant. Of these changes
the two following are the most conspicuous. The pith,
instead of being surrounded by a cylinder of small vascular cords, the diameter of which hardly exceeds its own,
as was the case in the one-year-old shoot-axis (fig. 9), is
now a mere speck in the middle of a huge mass of wood
many hundreds of times as broad as itself, and the cambium cylinder which was developed, as we saw, in the primary vascular bundles, is now a large (though still thin)
layer encircling this huge wood mass. Again, in place of
a delicate epidermis surrounding a soft, green, cellular
cortex, as we had in the young stem, there is here a hard,
brown, rugged bark, splitting off in thick ridges on the
outside.

The two chief series of change may be inferred from
comparing the two conditions, and taking into consideration all we have learnt so far. The pith is the same

pith as before, and it is the cambium cylinder which
has moved outwards, as it were, putting in all that
solid-looking timber as it did so. The epidermis and

FIG. 26.—Photograph of the transverse section of a log of
oak, about one-sixth natural size. The cortex and bark
are removed, and the outline is bounded by the cambium.
The pith appears as a mere dot in the centre; the medullary rays radiate from this, and the annual rings (about
forty in number) are arranged concentrically around
it. A large crack has formed along the plane of a medullary ray as the section dried. (Müller.)

the cortex of our young stem have disappeared, however, their place being taken by cork and bark. Closer
inspection will show that a series of layers of phloëm

H 2

have also been formed between these outer protective layers and the cambium.

We have now to obtain some ideas as to these curious processes of increase in thickness of the stems and branches.

The first thing to ensure this is to understand the constitution and behaviour of the cambium cylinder, for it is principally this tissue which brings about the changes we have to study.

We saw in Chapter IV. that the xylem of each primary vascular bundle is separated from the phloëm of the same bundle by a thin strand of cambium (figs. 9 and 12); we also saw that the bundles are arranged in a closed ring round the pith, and are in their turn surrounded by the primary cortex, each being separated laterally from its neighbours by a primary medullary ray. The next point to bear in mind is that these medullary rays (like the pith and cortex) are merely parts of the general cell-tissue, or fundamental tissue, through which the vascular bundles run upwards and downwards with a tangentially sinuous course from the leaves. The primary medullary rays, therefore, are merely spokes, as it were, joining the pith and cortex; and if we could remove the whole of the vascular bundles and epidermis from the young stem we should have left a solid cylinder of cells (pith) in the centre, a hollow cylinder (cortex) concentric to this, and a space between the two bridged over at numerous places by cellular spokes (medullary rays) radiating from the pith to the cortex. Each spoke is very thin from side

to side, and therefore stands out like a knife, with an
upper and a lower edge (fig. 27).

Now imagine the primary vascular bundles replaced.

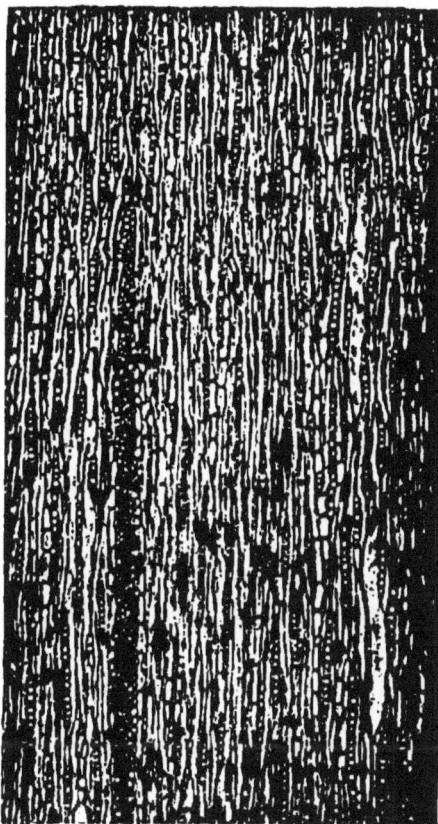

FIG. 27.—Tangential longitudinal section of oak wood,
magnified fifty diameters, and showing the transverse sections of the medullary rays, cut as they project towards
the observer. (Müller.)

The first change is that the cambium in the vascular
bundles becomes continuous across through the medul-

lary rays, and so forms a complete thin cylinder, concentric to the pith—from which it is separated by the
breadth of the xylem—and the cortex, from which it
is separated by the breadth of the phloëm.

The cells of this cambium cylinder go on dividing
continuously during the whole summer, until the
cylinder is, say, ten times as thick as it was before.
Now suppose it to rest during the winter and go on
again next season, and so on during each successive
period of growth. Obviously this would realise one
fact in the process we are considering—namely, that the
stem would grow in thickness year by year, its diameter
being increased by twice the thickness of the added
cylinder.

But to make the above supposition accord with the
facts, we must further picture to ourselves that when the
thickening cylinder has attained a certain thickness, a
large proportion of those of its cells which lie on the
inside—*i.e.* nearest the pith, and therefore abutting on
the xylem—lose their cambial nature and become converted into elements of the wood ; while a smaller proportion of those on the outer side (beneath the phloëm)
become new phloëm elements. In this way it will be
seen that the thin cylinder of active cambium cells
travels outwards ; ever receding radially further from the
pith, and leaving xylem between itself and the primary
vascular bundles next the pith, and ever driving outwards
the primary phloëm and cortex, adding new phloëm
elements (but in far less proportion) to the inside of the

phloëm. Each winter it pauses in this process, and each spring it renews its activity. Further peculiarities will be noticed as we proceed.

Now let us see what the cambium cells are, and how they change into new elements of the xylem and phloëm, &c., respectively.

Each cell of the cambium is a thin-walled prism, many times longer than broad or thick, and with its ends brought to an edge like that of a thick chisel, and so arranged that these edges run radially and fit in between those of cambium cells at higher and lower levels. As we have seen, the prism is oblong in transverse section. Each of these cells contains protoplasm and a nucleus, surrounding a sap-cavity, and they are nourished like other cells by the substances brought down from the leaves and up from the roots, taking what they need from the sap.

When a given cambium cell has taken into its protoplasm sufficient food materials, and has accomplished other life-processes under the action of oxygen, which it absorbs dissolved in the water of the sap, it grows larger, especially in the radial direction, and then it divides into two cells; then each of these may repeat these processes, and so on. At last the older ones can no longer grow and divide, but become changed into elements of the xylem or phloëm, according to their position. All the xylem thus produced by the cambium is called secondary xylem, and the phloëm secondary phloëm, and so on, to distinguish them from the primary structures found in the early stage.

I now proceed to some further details, which could only be rendered intelligible in the light of the preceding preliminary remarks.

After the cambium ring is once formed the daughter-cells cut off on the inside of the cambium always become transformed into one or more of the following elements :—

(1) Some cambium cells which lie on the radial continuation of a medullary ray undergo a few horizontal divisions across the long axis, and then simply pass over as constituents of a medullary ray ; as the cambium ring moves outwards, in consequence of the repeated formation of thickening rings, the periphery of the cylinder of course increases, and this allows of more space tangentially.　One consequence of this is the occasional and gradual widening of the medullary ray in process of lengthening : this takes place to a small extent only.　Another consequence of the increased space is the occasional interpolation of new medullary rays.　Radial rows of cambial cells at points which lie between the planes of two gradually diverging medullary rays suddenly commence to form new medullary rays.　Hence, as the wood mass increases in radial thickness, more and more of these interpolated medullary rays appear, cutting up the wood proper into partial sections.　In succeeding years the cambium keeps adding to the length of these rays, as it does to that of the older rays, and again forms new ones between as space increases.　In the same ring about thirteen

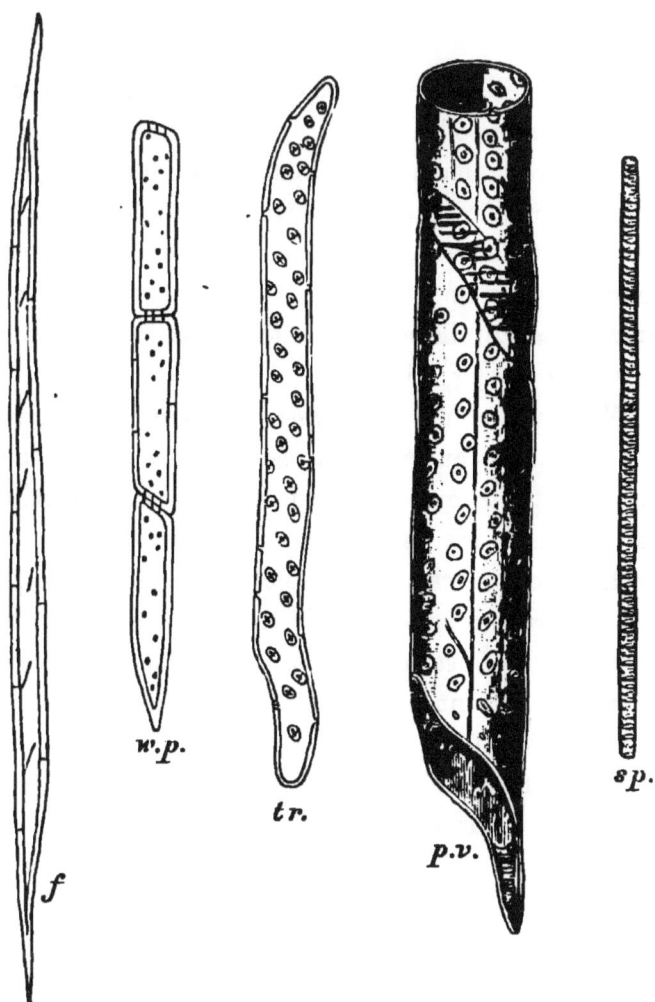

FIG. 28.—The various chief elements of the wood of the
oak, isolated by maceration, and highly magnified. *f*, a
fibre, distinguished by its thick walls, simple slit-like
pits, and no contents; *w.p*, part of a row of wood-parenchyma cells, with simple pits, and containing starch in
winter; *tr*, a tracheid, distinguished from the fibre
especially by its bordered pits; *p.v*, part of a rather large
pitted vessel, made up of communicating segments, each
of which corresponds to a tracheid, and has bordered pits
on its walls; *sp*, part of a spiral vessel.

rays to the millimetre may be counted on the transverse section of the wood.

(2) The cambium cells situated between the rays—except when they suddenly commence to form a new ray, as just described—pass over into one or more of the following elements of the wood proper—viz. wood parenchyma, libriform fibres, tracheids, segments of the vessels (*see* fig. 28).

When a cambium cell passes over into wood parenchyma it first undergoes a few horizontal divisions transverse to its long axis, and then we have a vertical row of five or six parenchymatous cells, the walls of which do not thicken much, but obtain small simple pits, and retain part of their living contents—protoplasm, nucleus, starch-forming corpuscles, &c.—and indeed present much resemblance to the cells of the medullary rays themselves.

When the cambial cell becomes transformed into a libriform fibre it does this simply by thickening its walls at the expense of the living contents, &c., which soon disappear. The cell undergoes no horizontal divisions, and probably elongates very slightly. The thickened walls become pitted with minute simple pits, and are stratified and eventually lignified.

In the case of the transformation of a cambial cell into a tracheid everything is essentially as described in the last paragraph, except that the diameter increases and the thickening walls become marked with bordered pits, quite similar to those of the pine, except that they are more numerous, are not confined to the radial walls, and they are not quite circular, but have an oval shape with a slit-like aperture to the border, the long axis of the slit being nearly transverse to the long axis of the tracheid.

In the conversion of cambium cells into vessels the chief point to note is that the vessel is essentially a vertical row of superposed tracheids—each of which has been developed from a cambium cell as just described —the oblique separating walls of which become almost entirely obliterated.   The markings, thickening, and want of contents are as in the case of tracheids, the chief difference being the more pronounced growth in diameter of the vessel segments, especially those formed in the spring wood.

It will readily be understood that the growth in diameter of these vessel elements exerts a disturbing effect on the radial arrangement of the other elements of the wood, and the displacements and compression of the latter are considerable and various, so that at length very little trace of the original order is observable.   It not unfrequently happens, however, that many successive rows of the fibres or tracheids are formed in the outer parts of the annual ring, and in such cases the original radial series can be detected.

There are several other points also to be noted in the development of secondary wood.   In the first place, the various elements do not maintain an exact vertical position, but may lean over both in the radial and in the

tangential directions. These slight displacements from
the vertical are chiefly due to the fact that the elements
—fibres, tracheids, and vertical groups of wood parenchyma—have not finished their growth in length when
they pass over from the cambial condition ; consequently
the pointed ends of the elongating fibres, &c., push
themselves between the ends of others which lie above
and below them, and a slight tilting from the vertical
results. This may be sufficient to produce a twisting of
the stems and branches which is visible even to the
unaided eye.

Another important point is that the length of the
elements, as well as their diameters, vary at different
periods in the life of the tree.

First as to the diameter. The fibres and tracheids
developed in the autumn have a relatively smaller
radial diameter than those formed earlier, and this, combined with the fact that those elements which develop
in the spring have the relatively largest diameters,
alone would suffice to mark the boundary between
any two annual rings. But the same holds good for
the vessels ; those formed in the spring wood are very
large compared with those formed later—the latter are
also more sparely developed—whence the contrast at the
boundary between the annual rings is intensified. With
the diminution in relative diameter of the tracheids and
fibres a corresponding increase in the thickness of their
walls is connected—a phenomenon which again intensi-
fies the contrast between adjacent annual rings.

But, in addition to these differences in diameter
within one and the same annual ring, a gradual increment in the average size of certain of the elements (both
in length and diameter) occurs as the tree becomes
older—in other words, the average width and length of
the elements increases year by year up to a certain age;
after reaching a definite size they enlarge no more.
These changes differ according to the part of the tree
concerned.   In the stem of the oak the chief changes
in this connection are :—

The fibres increase in length as follows, according to
Sanio's measurements:—While they average 0·42 mm. in
length in the first annual ring, they increase to 0·60 mm.
in the second, 0·74 mm. in the fourth, and go up to
1·22 mm. after a great age (130 years ?).   The tracheids
in the same annual rings were found to average 0·39,
0·43, 0·53, and 0·72 mm. respectively; and the individual
members or segments of the larger vessels averaged
0·25 mm. in the second annual ring, 0·26 mm. in the
fourth, and 0·36 mm. in the three outer rings.   The
mean radial diameter of these vessels also increased : in
the third year it was 0·08 mm., and it rose year by year
until in the sixth year the definitive width of 0·31 to
0·33 mm. was attained.   After this the width of these
vessels is practically constant.   These increments in
size appear to take place after the element has passed
out of the strictly cambial condition.

The passage of the older wood in the centre of the
stem into the condition known as 'heart-wood' (dura-

men) as opposed to 'sap-wood' (alburnum) is not
attended with any profound anatomical changes; the
chief alterations are of the nature of infiltration by
foreign chemical substances, and alteration in the phy-
sical properties of the cell-walls and in the contents.
These changes are somewhat sudden, and the fact that
starch ceases to be deposited in this altered wood helps
to indicate that the change is one of degradation—the
cells of the softer tissues have ceased to be 'alive,' and
the 'heart' commences to undergo degradation.   At
the same time, although we must regard the 'heart' as
dead, it is very resistant, perhaps owing to the preser-
vative action of infiltrated bodies.

A remarkable phenomenon which may be noticed
here is the filling up of the older large vessels with
tyloses.   These are thin-walled, bladder-like vesicles
projecting into the cavity of the vessel from the bordered
pits, and are, in fact, due to the protrusion into the cavity
of the thin-walled parenchyma cells, which drive the pit
membrane in and then swell up.   At the planes of
contact between various tyloses from opposite points on
the wall of the vessel the tyloses are flattened, and the
appearance is very like that of a parenchymatous tissue
(fig. 29, d).   When young the tyloses are found to
contain a nucleus, protoplasm, and cell-sap, and they are
known to form division membranes and divide like cells
of the pith or cortex; later on they lose their contents
and form a sort of packing in the by this time function-
less vessel.

During the whole time of the activity of the cambium ring and the formation of wood on its interior, it must not be forgotten that the outer rows of cambial cells are passing over into the tissue known as bast or secondary phloëm (also called secondary cortex); the chief differences in the process being (1) that much

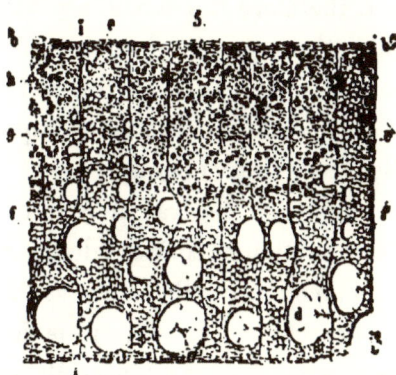

FIG. 29.—A small piece of one annual ring of old oak wood (magnified twenty diameters). *a*, boundary of the autumn wood of the preceding (older) ring; *b*, that between the zone shown and the next youngest ring. In the annual ring shown the spring wood begins with large vessels, *c* and *d*, some with tyloses, *d*, in them, and passes gradually into autumn wood, with smaller vessels, *e, e*, and more tracheids and fibres, *g*. Only small medullary rays, *i*, are shown. (Hartig.)

less phloëm than xylem is formed; (2) that the elements do not become lignified; and (3) that the disturbances in the arrangement of the elements are more profound from the continued pressure exerted upon them between the resistant wood and the elastic periderm and bark, on the one hand, and the increased extension tangentially which it undergoes as the

thickening mass of wood drives it outwards, on the
other. The other differences chiefly concern the individual elements now to be described.

All that was said of the medullary rays in the wood
applies also to those in the bast; the cambium in keeping open or originating new medullary rays does so on
both sides, and therefore the medullary rays are to be
traced radially through the cambium from wood to
cortex. The rays in the bast are termed ' bast rays;'
the broader ones contain isolated groups of sclerotic
cells and cells containing crystals.

The changes which the radial rows of cells on the
exterior of the cambium zone undergo to form the
elements of the secondary phloëm are as follows :—

(1) Bast parenchyma (fig. 17, *bp*) is developed, like
the wood parenchyma, from cambium cells which undergo
a few transverse divisions and then pass over as longitudinal groups of cells, which retain their living contents,
&c. From these longitudinal groups, accompanying the
sieve-tubes as parallel series, they are called companion
cells (cambiform cells).

(2) Sieve-tubes (fig. 18, *bp*), which may be regarded
as homologous with the vessels of the wood, and, like
those, are constituted of series of segments. Each segment corresponds to a cambium cell, and is obliquely
tapering at the end where it fits on to another segment.
These dividing septa are not completely broken through,
as in the case of the wood-vessels, however, but are
pierced by a grating-like series of holes (the sieve)

through which the protoplasmic and other contents of
the contiguous segments pass uninterruptedly. Similar
sieve-plates occur on the lateral walls of the segments
also. The walls are not thickened and not lignified, and
thus the morphological similarities between the sieve-
tubes of the bast and the vessels of the wood (which only
contain air and water, have their septa absorbed, and
their walls lignified and covered with bordered and simple
pits) depends almost entirely on the similar development. The sieve-pores are very fine, and easily overlooked.

(3) The bast fibres (figs. 17 and 18, b), which are homologous with the libriform fibres of the wood, and are developed in the same way from single cells of the cambium.
They are short, blunt, very thick-walled fibres, grouped
in strands which appear on the transverse section of the
bast as tangential bands 2–4 deep, alternating (in the
radial direction) with broader bands of sieve-tubes and
parenchyma. These bands of fibres (hard bast) are
accompanied at their outer and inner boundaries by
parenchyma-like cells arranged in vertical rows, each
of which contains a large simple crystal of calcium
oxalate embedded in yellowish substance, and the walls
of which are slightly sclerotic. Similar vertical series
of cells are found in the soft bast, but they contain
compound (clustered) crystals of the same salt (figs. 17
and 18, e).

The soft bast also contains scattered roundish
groups of short sclerenchyma cells, the thickened walls

of which are traversed by very numerous pit-canals; cells containing crystals also accompany these groups.

In consequence of the above arrangements the secondary cortex presents a more or less stratified appearance on the transverse section, the strata consisting chiefly of alternate tangential layers of hard bast and soft bast (fig. 17); the elements of the latter also showing a decided tendency to be arranged in layers.

After the first year the young stem or branches covered with thin periderm are seen to be dotted with lenticels or cortical pores. Structures similar in every respect and subserving the same function—viz. the exchange of gases with the environment—are formed on the roots as soon as the periderm is developed.

The lenticel is a local interruption of the periderm, where the cells are loosened so as to allow air to pass between the loosened cells into the intercellular spaces between the cortical cells. Each lenticel may be described as a biconvex projecting swelling of the periderm, the swelling being caused by the increased radial diameter of the loosened cells. This is the condition during the spring and summer, but in the winter the cork-cambium is continuous across beneath the lenticel, and forms periderm in an uninterrupted sheet, to be ruptured again at the lenticel during the formation and swelling of the looser cells (complementary or packing cells) in the following spring. These loose packing-cells are at first quite similar to young cork-cells, and are developed as such, but they loosen and round off,

and their cell-walls do not become completely suberised
for a long time, but are capable of swelling: in fact, the
rounding off depends on the absorption of water by the
cellulose walls and contents.   The outer parts of the
older lenticel openings are thrown off with the bark-
scales, but the inner parts remain, and can be found
between the scales in older branches, in the fissures.

The first points of origin of lenticels are usually
beneath the stomata, and the lenticels may be regarded
as devices for prolonging the passages of the stomata
through the thickening periderm year by year.   The
cortical cells beneath the stoma become meristematic—in
effect they continue the phellogen below the stoma, only
they divide less regularly and in all directions.   The
daughter-cells thrown off externally swell up and pro-
trude, driving the stomatic cells outwards and apart, and
emerging between the ruptured guard-cells as the first
packing-tissue.   The phellogen or cambium of the
lenticel forms phelloderm on its interior in continuation
of that formed by the rest of the cork-cambium.   The
protruding packing-cells dry up eventually, and form the
powdery substance seen between the gaping lips of
older lenticels.   In the autumn the cells formed by the
meristem below the packing-cells do not separate, but
are suberised and closely and radially arranged like the
rest of the cork : in fact, they continue the cork layer
as a closing layer beneath the lenticel, thus protecting
the tissues beneath through the winter.   In the following spring new layers of loose, swelling packing-cells

are developed again, and these absorb water and bulge, bursting the closing layer and reopening the lenticel for the season. As the branch ages and its surface increases new lenticels are developed between the earlier ones, and, of course, with no reference to stomata.

The exterior of the very young stem or branch is smooth or slightly pubescent, the green colour gradually passing into a silver-grey as the periderm develops, and in a few years (when the shoot is from five to twenty years old, or thereabouts) the gradually thickening bark is shining and turning browner, flecked with lenticels and lichens. Later still the bark is rugged, brown, and fissured, and usually covered with small lichens and fungi. Bark begins to exfoliate at about the thirtieth year.

The epidermis cracks and peels off when the twigs are a year old, and shreds of the dead membrane may be detected on the outside of the young cork, which begins to form very early during the first year. It is, in fact, owing to the impervious nature of this cork that the epidermis dies, and to the stretching of the cortex as the stem grows in thickness that the dead membrane cracks and peels off (*see* figs. 17 and 18).

The first indication of the development of the cork is the conversion of the sub-epidermal layer of cortex-cells into a meristem—*i.e.* the cells become capable of active growth and division.

Each cell of the layer referred to may be termed an initial cell of the cork-cambium (or phellogen), and the layer may be called the initial layer. This layer behaves essentially like the cambium of a fibro-vascular bundle, except that its daughter-cells become cork and phelloderm instead of phloëm and xylem.

The first event to notice is that each of the initial cells grows radially, and divides by a tangential wall into an inner cell nearest the axis of the branch and an outer cell nearer the epidermis; the outer cell becomes forthwith a cork-cell—*i.e.* its contents die and mostly disappear, and the cellulose cell-wall becomes suberised —the inner cell remains capable of repeating the process. But this is not the only case. After the division, as before, of the initial cell, it may happen that the *inner* cell becomes transformed into a collenchymatous cortical cell containing chlorophyll, and it is the outer of the daughter-cells which retains the meristem character and acts again as a phellogen cell, cutting off daughter-cells sometimes on one side and at others on the other. Thus, in the oak, the phellogen gives rise to permanent tissue on both sides of the initial layer: those cells which lie on the inside become *phelloderm* (cortical cells), those on the outside become transformed into *phellem* (cork). The three tissues, phelloderm, phellogen, and phellem, are called the periderm.

It is obvious that the cork-cambium, by thus adding to the cortical parenchyma, is gradually driven radially outwards from the centre of the stem. This means that it obtains room to extend tangentially, and it does this by its cells occasionally dividing by walls perpendicular

to the far more numerous tangential walls. It is also
easy to see that the cork-cells must be arranged in
radial rows, and this arrangement is very conspicuous
(fig. 18). The earlier cork-cells have very thin walls,
later ones have the walls thicker.

After the development of the first layer of cork the
stretched epidermis dies, and forms simply a dead membrane outside the thin cork. In succeeding years
layers of phellogen are formed annually beneath the
older ones, and thus the cork layers increase. Moreover,
since the successive layers cut out thin, scale-like areas
of cortex, trapping them, as it were, between the present
and the preceding cork, the thickening corky covering
is stratified—consists of successive and obliquely over-
laying thin sheets of dead cortex and cork proper (fig.
30). Again, since the increase in thickness of the stem
or branch is continually driving these corky and dead
structures outwards, they at length crack, and form the
fissured bark found on older parts. Bark is thus seen
to be something more than cork, or even periderm, and
it is defined to be all the dead tissues cut out by the
phellogen.

It is also to be noticed that the successive phellogen
layers of different years are not concentric, but the new
ones cut the old ones at acute angles (fig. 30), thus cutting out scale-like areas of cortex ; the consequence of
this is the formation of the very irregular scales of bark
thrown off from the older stems and branches of the oak.
It follows from what has been said that in older trees the

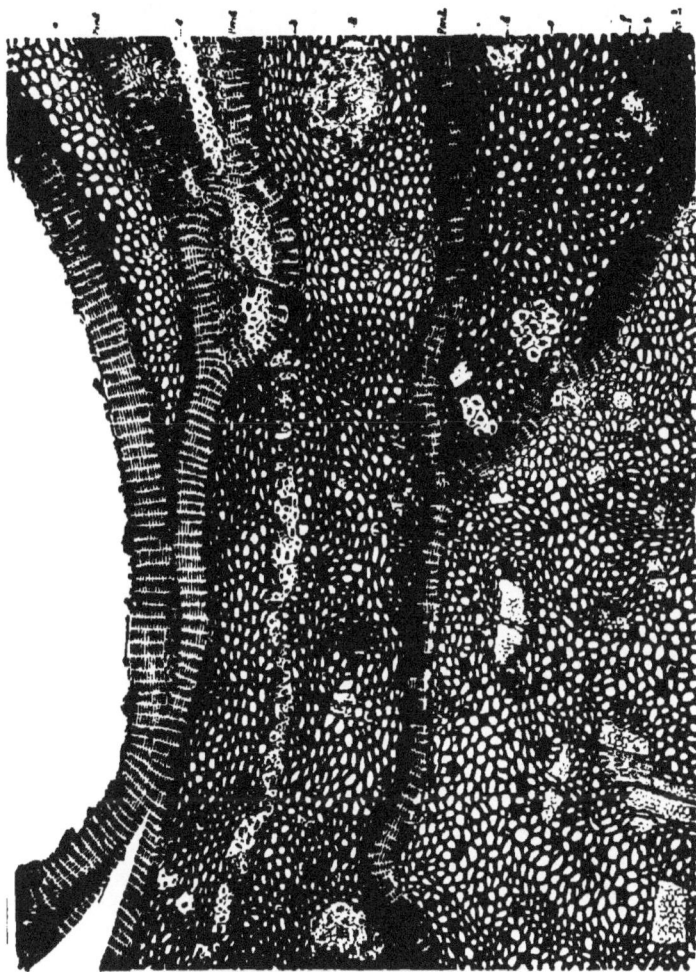

FIG. 30.—Transverse section of bark of oak. The successive cork-layers (*Perid*) cut out masses of the cortex, and since everything which is thus separated from the underlying tissues dies, scales of bark, consisting of various kinds of tissues—sclerenchyma, *d*; parenchyma, *e*; bast-fibres, *e*; crystal cells, *f*, &c.—are cut off periodically. All that lies outside the innermost sheet of cork is comprised under the term bark. (Kny.)

phellogen layers may be formed so far down in the cortex that they cut out tissues of the secondary cortex— *i.e.* phloëm and bast fibres. It is, of course, this gradual exfoliation of the cut-out areas of bark that explains the relative thinness of the bark in very old stems and branches; the whole of the primary cortex, and most of that formed from the cambium, have been thrown off as bark long before.

CHAPTER IX

THE TREE (*continued*). INFLORESCENCE AND FLOWERS—
FRUIT AND SEED

THE oak flowers in May in this country, the young
inflorescences developing as the leaves unfold. The
flowers are unisexual, both male and female appearing
on the same branches—*i.e.* the tree is monœcious—and
even on the same twigs of the current year. The rule
is that the apical bud of a last year's twig produces
a few male inflorescences from between the axils of the
upper scales, and then grows out into a green twig
bearing about six to ten normal leaves, the female inflorescences arising from the axils of two or three of the
upper leaves (figs. 31 and 32). Lateral buds below the
terminal bud of the last year's twig usually produce male
inflorescences only—a phenomenon in accordance with
their feeble development generally. Thus the male inflorescences are produced first—a common occurrence in
forest trees.

Since the inflorescences arise from the axils of
leaves, their arrangement accords with the phyllotaxis

of the tree—*i.e.* $\frac{2}{5}$—so far as it goes.   It should be
borne in mind that the bud-scales are *stipules*.

The male inflorescences hang down from between
the bud-scales as simple catkin-like spikes, each bearing about a dozen flowers.   Each male flower springs

Fig. 31.—A sprig of oak in May, with the pendent male
   catkins below, and the minute spikes of female flowers
   just showing above.   (Th. Hartig.)

from the axil of a tiny scale-like bract, and consists of
a shallow perianth, unequally divided into about five to
seven small linear-lanceolate lobes, enclosing about five
to twelve stamens; there is no trace of an ovary.   The
number of lobes of the perianth varies, as also does the

number of stamens; the former are covered with short hairs.

Each of the stamens consists of a slender thread (filament) bearing on its top a four-chambered swollen anther. This contains a yellow dust, the pollen, composed of round grains (pollen grains), each with three thinner spots in its otherwise thick wall. Each of these pollen grains consists of a membrane enclosing nucleated protoplasm and food materials. When ripe the wind blows the pollen as it scatters from the dangling stamens, and some of the grains reach the stigmas of the female flowers; here they germinate, each pollen grain sending a delicate pollen tube down the style into the ovary of the flower. This process of application of the pollen grains to the stigma is termed pollination, and depends on the wind.

The female inflorescences are also spikes (fig. 32, A), but they bear only one to five flowers, and stand off from the axils of the foliage leaves. In the commonest English variety (*Q. pedunculata*) the spikes are rather long, obliquely erect, and the flowers are scattered on the upper end of the rachis of the spike; in other varieties the flowers are more clustered in the axils of the leaves. Here, as in one or two other details, minute differences are apparent in different individuals; similar trifling differences are met with in the structure of the male flowers.

Each female flower springs (like the male) from the axil of a small bract : in other respects it is very unlike the male flower. In the first place, the ovary is inferior, being sunk in and fused into a six-partite perigone, the teeth of which project some distance up and surround a trifid stigma (figs. 33 and 34, c). One of the lobes of the perigone will be found opposite to the bract; the three

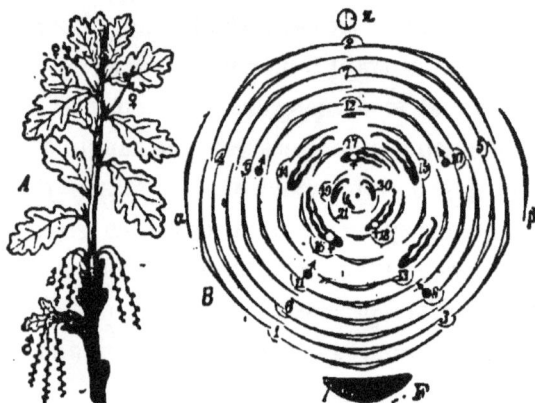

FIG. 32.—A. Flowering twig and inflorescences, male (♂) and female (♀), semi-diagrammatic. B. Diagram of plan of a similar but lateral twig. F. Leaf from axil of which the twig arises: *x*, parent stem; *a* and *β*, bracts. The numbers 1-11 denote pairs of stipules acting as bud-scales, some with male inflorescences (♂) springing from between them; the continued numbers 12-21 also denote pairs of stipules, but these have their accompanying leaves, with or without female inflorescences (♀) in the axils. (Eichler.)

lobes of the stigma are superposed on three alternate (outer) lobes of the perigone.

There is yet a further covering to the female flower. The somewhat irregular margins of a minute cup-like investment are to be seen arising from beneath and around the perigone: this is the scaly cupula, the future

'cup' in which the 'acorn' is inserted (fig. 34, m).   If
the young female flower is carefully bisected longitudinally this cupule will be seen to consist of a ring of
tissue, arising from beneath the ovary, and with its
margin notched into scales.   As the ovule enlarges
the minute scales. become more numerous, new ones
arising at the inner margin of the up-growing cupule.

A transverse section
across the female flower
at a slightly later period
shows that the inferior
ovary is divided into
three chambers (*loculi*),
each corresponding to
one of the lobes of the
stigma, and each con-
taining two ovules (fig.
34).   These ovules are
inserted at the upper
part of the inner angle
of the chamber, and
thus   hang   down   in

FIG. 33.—A group of female flowers
(slightly magnified).   Each has a
spreading stigma above and the
commencing cupule below, and
arises from the axil of a pointed
bract.   (Th. Hartig.)

pairs.   A curious point arises here.   It seems that at
the period when the female flower has just opened,
but has not yet received any pollen on its stigma,
neither the ovules nor the chambers are as yet formed,
and the segments of the perigone spring from the lower
portion of the flower, and this condition is not altered
until pollination occurs; then the tissue below the

stigma becomes the three-chambered ovary sunk in the perigone.

The pollination takes place in May–June, and fertilisation soon afterwards; in July the young acorns can

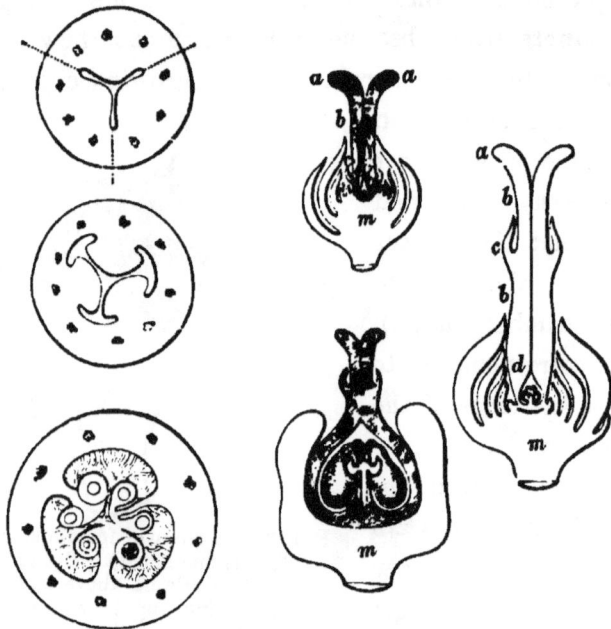

FIG. 34.—Female flower in section. To the left three transverse sections through the young ovary; the lower one showing the three placentas, each with two ovules. To the right, three longitudinal median sections through the whole flower at successive periods. *a*, stigma; *b*, carpel; *c*, perianth; *d*, cavity of ovary with ovules; *m*, the cupule. (Th. Hartig.)

be made out peeping from the cupules in which they had hitherto been enclosed. The acorn reaches its full size towards the end of September, and ripens and falls in October. When ripe the acorn is, as we have seen, an ovoid, smooth, olive-brown nut, with the broad end inserted into the cupule, and the narrower, somewhat tapering end projecting free.

It will be interesting, in the light of the foregoing remarks, to examine one of the stronger lateral buds of the oak towards the end of April, before it unfolds. A transverse section of such a bud shows the following structures :—In the centre is the axis of the young shoot, represented by the small central dot in the diagram (fig. 32, B). Surrounding this are about eight to ten green leaves in section, and folded on their midribs in such a way that the two halves of the upper surface are face to face and somewhat crumpled ; some of these are turned so that their edges are directed one way, others with them directed the other.

Each of these leaves has a pair of small stipules, also cut across, and rather difficult to identify (fig. 32, 12–20). Some of the foliage leaves bear female inflorescences in their axils, as indicated by the sign ♀ in the figure. Following on these stipulate leaves are a number of pairs of larger stipules, devoid of foliage leaves and constituting the bud-scales (fig. 32, 1–11). Some of these bear male inflorescences (♂) between them —*i.e.* in the position corresponding to the axil of the leaf.

It will be understood that in this diagram the parts are all represented on a ground-plan, but that as the bud opens the inner leaves and stipules are on higher levels than the outer scales. In fact, proceeding in the order of the numerals, we pass in an ascending spiral

from the outermost lower pair (1) of scales (stipules) to
the innermost upper pair (21) with their leaf.

If we suppose the female inflorescences removed, the
above diagram will serve to represent the lateral buds
which develop male inflorescences only, or if we suppose the three bracts F, *a*, and *β* away, it would serve
for a terminal bud.

Each single female flower stands in the axil of a
minute scale on the floral axis, as said, and its general
structure has been described. When the pollen grains
have been dusted on to the trifid stigma, about the end
of May or beginning of June, each grain germinates
and sends a minute tube down the style, and this pollen-
tube soon reaches the cavity of the ovary, and its end
becomes applied to one of the ovules. While the
pollen-tube is descending the style, the ovules have
arisen as minute cellular outgrowths from the angles of
the three chambers of the ovary (fig. 34, *d*). There are
two in each chamber. Each ovule is at first a mere
solid lump of cells (*nucellus*), which curves and becomes
enveloped in two thin investing layers, called integuments, as shown in the figures A–D (fig. 35). Inside
the solid nucellus, *n*, of the ovule there soon arises a
small cavity filled with nucleated protoplasm, and termed
the embryo-sac, *e*, because the embryo is to be developed in it.

This embryo-sac contains, among other structures,
a minute, nucleated, naked mass of protoplasm, called
the oosphere, or egg-cell. The pollen-tube has carried

down in its apex also a nucleated mass of protoplasm, and it passes this over into the egg-cell in the embryo-

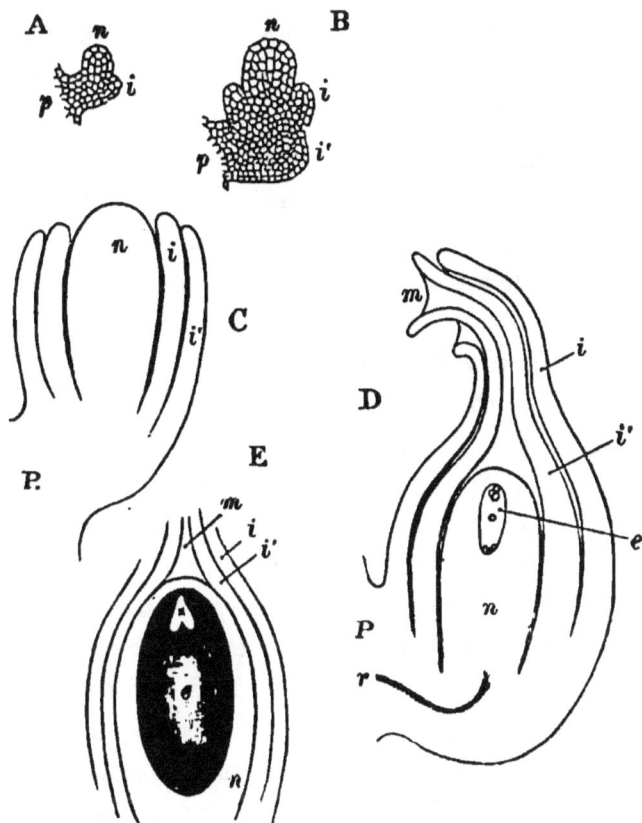

FIG. 35.—Various stages in the development of the ovule. *n*, nucellus; *i*, *i'*, integuments; *p*, point of attachment to placenta; *e*, embryo-sac; *r*, vascular cord supplying ovule; *m*, micropyle; *x*, young embryo. (Partly after Th. Hartig.)

sac; the union of the nucleus from the pollen-tube with the nucleus of the egg-cell constitutes the act of

K

fertilisation, and the fertilised egg-cell is now termed the oospore, and at once begins to grow into the embryo.

It would be very interesting to describe at length all the remarkable details of these processes, and their morphological meaning in the light of modern biology, but the limits and purpose of this little book will not admit of that, and I must content myself with this brief *résumé*.

During this process of fertilisation the cupule has grown up like a scaly wall round the ovary (fig. 34), and the tip of the latter is seen peeping out from its orifice.

We are now in a position to understand generally the changes that convert the female flower into the cupped acorn. The fertilised oospore becomes the embryo (fig. 35, *x*); it grows at the expense of the contents of the embryo-sac, and develops a radicle, a plumule, and two relatively large cotyledons, which soon become so big that they occupy the whole space in the sac (fig. 36). Moreover, the embryo-sac increases to make more room for this growing embryo. And now comes in a curious point. We saw that the ovary consisted of three chambers, each containing two ovules; each of these six ovules also had its embryo-sac, containing an egg-cell, &c., and each of the total of six egg-cells may be fertilised by the contents of so many pollen-tubes coming from pollen grains on the stigmas. But the rule is that five of the ovules with their contents perish at an early period, because one strong one takes the lead in development, and starves the rest by taking all the available nourishment to itself. Consequently the advancing ovary is soon filled by *one* avule—the other five and two of the chambers being pressed to one side by it.

In a few weeks the ovary and its cupule have increased considerably in size, and the one successful ovule, with the rapidly developing embryo in the

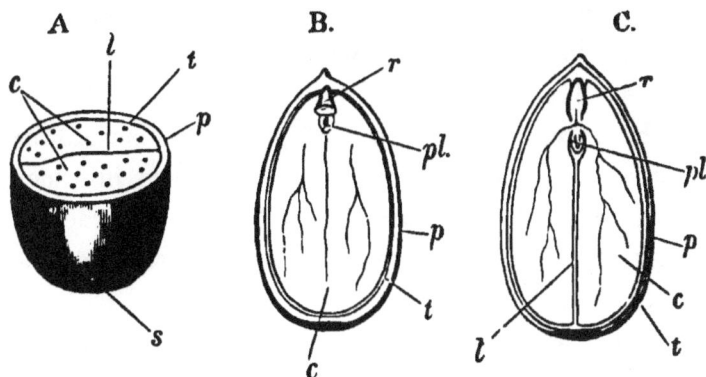

FIG. 36.—Sections of acorns in three planes at right angles to one another. A, transverse; B, longitudinal in the plane of the cotyledons (*l*); C, longitudinal across the plane of the cotyledons; *c*, cotyledons; *t*, testa; *p*, pericarp; *s*, scar, and *r*, radicle; *pl*, plumule. The radicle, plumule, and cotyledons together constitute the embryo. The embryonic tissue is at *r* and *pl*. The dots in A, and the delicate veins in B and C are the vascular bundles.

embryo-sac in its interior, occupies nearly the whole of its cavity; the remains of the two aborted chambers and the five unsuccessful ovules being traceable as tiny, shrivelled remnants in one corner. The walls of the ovary then gradually change into the polished brown walls (pericarp) of the fruit; the walls of the ovule become the coat (testa) of the seed; and the embryo

developed from the fertilised egg-cell fills up the interior
of the latter, as described in Chapter II.

The ripe fruit is the acorn, and we may regard it
apart from the cupule ; it contains the seed.

The acorn is an egg-shaped, nut-like fruit (*glans*),
about 18 mm. long and 8-10 mm. broad (fig. 36);
the apex is somewhat pointed with a hard remnant of
the stigma, the base is broader, and marked with the
circular scar which denotes where it was inserted in the
cupule. The trifid character of the stigma can often be
observed even on the ripe fruit, which is smooth (or
with fine longitudinal striæ) and olive-brown in colour
when ripe. The ripe acorn may thus be regarded as
consisting of the pericarp (to which the calyx or perianth is fused) and the seed.

The pericarp (fig. 36, *p*) is a thin, hard shell, comprised of four layers :—(1) An epidermis of small,
cuboidal cells with their external walls much thickened
(fig. 37, E). (2) Four or five series of very thick-walled
and pitted sclerenchyma cells (fig. 37, 1). (3) Then
follow numerous rows of thin-walled parenchyma cells,
comprising the chief thickness of the pericarp (fig. 37).
It is in this tissue that the small vascular bundles
supplying the pericarp run, and here and there nests
of sclerenchyma cells are scattered. The parenchyma
cells may contain minute starch grains, in addition to
the remains of chlorophyll corpuscles, even when ripe ;
they also contain tannin, and, here and there, crystals
of calcium oxalate. (4) The internal epidermis consists
of elongated cells in one layer.

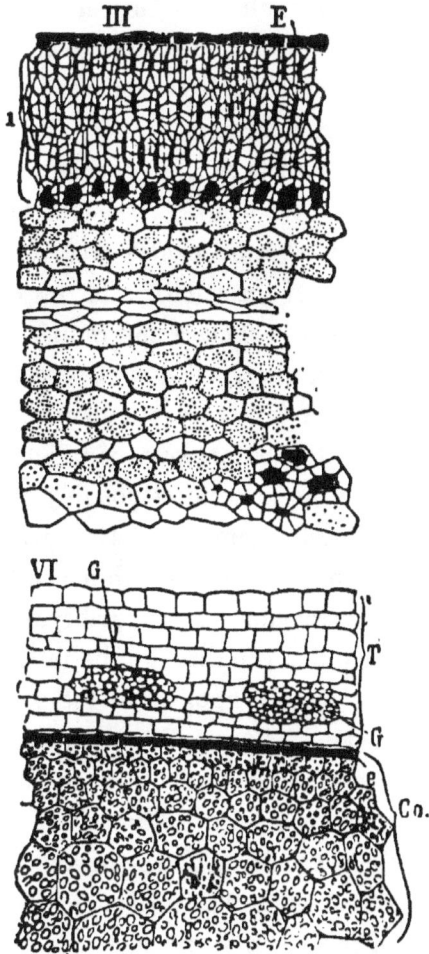

FIG. 37.—Transverse sections of the pericarp (III.) and
seed (VI.) of the oak. E, epidermis; i, thick layer of
sclerenchyma. Under this come the parenchyma cells,
with a few sclerenchyma cells here and there. T, testa
of seed; G, vascular bundles; e, the outer layer or epidermis of the cotyledon; Co, thin-walled cells of cotyledons (cf. figs. 35 and 36) filled with starch, &c.
(Harz.)

The seed proper fills up the entire cavity enclosed by the fruit-wall above described. It consists of a relatively very thin testa, or seed-coat, closely enveloping the large, straight embryo (fig. 36, *t*). At the broad end the funicle can be observed attaching the seed to the base of the acorn; it is inserted laterally, and traces of the aborted ovules may sometimes be found at the point of insertion. The vessels from the funiculus branch at the chalaza and ramify in the testa.

The testa is a shining, pale-brown or yellowish skin, consisting only of a few rows of cuboidal, thin-walled parenchyma cells, the outer rows of which may be the integuments, and the innermost possibly belong to the remains of the nucellus; or the latter may be represented by the outer portion of the thin membrane which includes all that remains of the embryo-sac. A few feeble vascular bundles run through the testa (fig. 37, G).

The testa is closely applied to the surface of the two stout cotyledons. These fill up by far the greater part of the space enclosed by the thin testa and pericarp, and their shape is almost described in saying that. Each is a colourless, hard, plano-convex body, face to face with the other by the flat surface (fig. 36); a transverse section of the acorn shows each cotyledon occupying half the circle. At the more pointed end of the acorn these two cotyledons will be found to be joined to the very small embryo (plumule and radicle) by what will on germination lengthen into very short stalks (petioles), but which are at present mere bridges of tissue, across which minute vascular bundles run from the embryo into the cotyledons. If the shell-like investments described above are removed from the embryo, it is then possible to gently separate the cotyledons and see the minute plumule and radicle to which they are joined (fig. 36); on removing one cotyledon the plumule will be seen embedded in a slight depression at the base. At this point there is a little room to spare, not quite filled up by the radicle and plumule; a minute remnant of endosperm may occasionally be found here, not having been entirely absorbed by the developing embryo.

The cotyledons and embryo are composed of a delicate epidermis enclosing the whole (fig. 37, e), and very thin-walled cells forming the main mass of tissue in which the vascular bundles run. These bundles are scattered in the thickness of the cotyledons, ready to convey fluids to and fro on germination, and already contain lignified vessels in the xylem and sieve-tubes in the phloëm.

The iso–diametric, closely-packed cells of the cotyledons are filled with reserve materials, consisting of large quantities of starch grains embedded in proteids and tannin. Here and there are scattered cells filled with brown pigments and containing tannin; some cells also contain oil-drops. Traces of sugar (quercite), certain bitter principles, acids, and mineral substances also occur in the tissues.

CHAPTER X

OAK TIMBER—ITS STRUCTURE AND TECHNOLOGICAL

PECULIARITIES

It is now time to look at the timber of the oak as a material, and to examine its technical properties from the various points of view of those who employ such material. Oak timber may be described as follows :—

(1) *Appearance and Structure.*—Pith pentangular, 1 to 4 mm. diameter, whitish at first, and then browner, formed of small, thick-walled cells.

Sap-wood narrow and yellowish-white; heart-wood varies in shades of greyish or yellow brown (fawn colour) to reddish or very dark brown. It darkens on exposure, and works to   glossy surface if healthy.

Annual rings well marked by the one to four lines of large vessels in the spring wood, whence radiate outwards tongue-like and branched groups of smaller and smaller vessels, tracheids, and cells, in a groundwork of darker fibres. Indistinct peripheral lines of parenchyma are also visible, especially in the broader annual rings. The annual rings are slightly undulating, bending outwards between the large medullary rays (fig. 38).

Medullary rays of two kinds, a smaller number of very broad, shining ones, from ½ to 1 mm., or even a centimetre or more apart, and very numerous (about

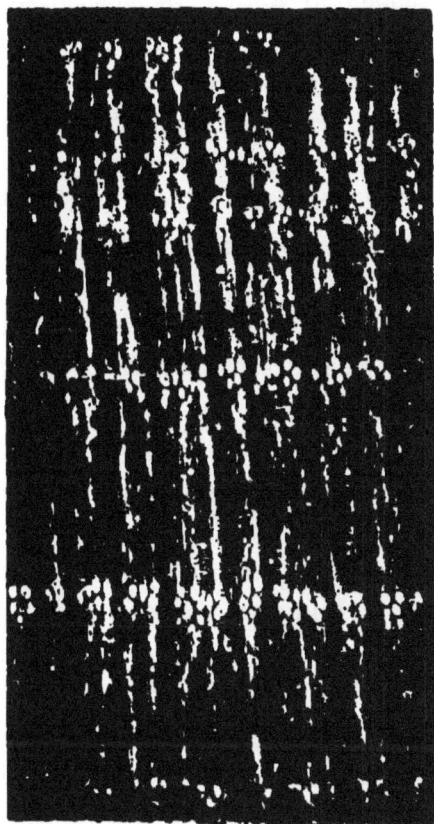

FIG. 38.—Transverse section of wood of oak (magnified five diameters), showing five annual rings, as denoted by the large vessels of the spring wood; the vessels become smaller in the summer and autumn wood, and are arranged in tongue-like groups. Nine broad medullary rays are shown, the rest are very narrow (*cf.* fig. 27). The rest of the section is filled with tracheids, fibres, and wood-parenchyma. (Müller.)

twelve per mm.) fine ones between them, which undulate between the vessels. In slowly-grown, close wood there is no vestige of radial arrangement left.

In the tangential section the small medullary rays are seen to consist each of a vertical row of a few cells, the large ones having numerous cells (*see* fig. 27).

Wood-parenchyma cells broader than small medullary rays, and the colour is chiefly due to pigment in these wood- and ray-cells. The wood-cells are pitted with oblique, slit-shaped, simple pits.

The vessels have bordered pits, and the septa are perforated each by one large circular opening. The smaller vessels have delicate spirals on their walls as well as bordered pits.

Nördlinger says that pith-flecks occur occasionally.

It is impossible to distinguish between the wood of the varieties *pedunculata* and *sessiliflora*.

(2) Its density varies considerably. Taking the weight of a given volume of water as unity, the weight of an equal volume of oak timber may weigh from 0·633 when air-dry to 1·280 when fresh cut. We may take the average density of green—*i.e.* newly-felled—oak, with all its sap present, as about 1·075, and that of the seasoned wood as about 0·78.

It must be borne in mind, however, that these weights refer to the wood as a structure—that is, a complex of vessels and cells, &c., containing air and liquids —and do not give the specific gravity of the wood substance itself. The latter may be obtained by driving

off all the air and water from the wood, and is found to
be 1·56, compared with an equal volume of water taken
as unity. It is the varying quantities of this wood substance, and of air and water in the cavities, which make
the density of different pieces of oak vary so much.

(3) The proportion of sap contained in the cavities of
the vessels, cells, &c., of course differs at different times.
In the spring, just as the buds are opening, the quantity
of water increases more and more up to about July, when
the maximum is attained; the proportion of water to
solids then sinks until October, when the leaves fall;
it increases again up to Christmas-tide, and then sinks
to the minimum in the coldest part of the winter. The
proportion of water to the total weight of the felled
wood may vary from 22 to 39 per cent.

(4) Obviously the loss of water on drying causes
shrinkage of the wood, and although oak shrinks very
little in the direction of its length (0·028 to 0·435 per
cent.), the effect is very marked in other directions. In
the radial direction—*i.e.* in the direction of the medullary rays—it may shrink from 1 to 7·5 per cent. of its
measurement when first felled; and in the direction
vertical to this—*i.e.* parallel to a tangent to the cylindrical
stem—the variation is from 0·8 to 10·6 per cent. Of
course, green oak shrinks much more than seasoned and
older wood, the process of seasoning being, in point of
fact, the period of chief shrinkage. It is said that wood
from the variety *sessiliflora* shrinks more than that of
the variety *pedunculata*, but it may be doubted how far

the difference would hold if sufficiently numerous comparisons were made.

(5) Swelling may be regarded as complementary to shrinkage. It has been found that if oak wood is allowed to absorb water until thoroughly saturated it will increase from 0·13 to 0·4 per cent. in length, and be distended radially from 2·66 to 3·9 per cent., or tangentially 5·59 to 7·55 per cent., according to age and condition, young wood swelling more than old. It has also been found that the total volume increased from 5·5 to 7·9 per cent., and the weight from 60 to 91 per cent., on complete saturation.

(6) *Elasticity and Tenacity.*—Oak is very elastic, and easily bent if steamed, and it does not readily splinter. When pulled in a direction parallel to the length of the structure the absolute tenacity = 2·23 to 14·51 kgr.—*i.e.* it took a pull equal to this weight per 1 sq. mm. of section to pull the wood asunder.

The limit of elasticity corresponds to a load of 2·72 to 3·5 kgr., according to various authorities, the specimen lengthening $\frac{1}{430}$th in the former case.

The modulus of elasticity is given as 826 to 1,030 kgr., and the breaking limit as 4·66 to 6·85.

When the pull is in a direction across the length of the fibres, the results differ according as the load is applied so as to act radially or tangentially.

When acting radially the modulus of elasticity is given as 188·7 kgr., and the breaking limit as 0·582 kgr.

When acting parallel to a tangent the modulus of

elasticity = 129·8 kgr., and the breaking limit 0·406 kgr.

The absolute tenacity in the transverse direction is given as 0·44 to 0·61 kgr.

In the case where pressures are applied in the direction of the length .of the fibres the limit of elasticity = 2·09 to 2·22 kgr.; the modulus of elasticity, 933 to 1,250 kgr.; and the absolute resistance, 2·58 to 3·64 kgr.

Flexibility.—The limit of elasticity = 1·77 to 2·71 kgr.; modulus of elasticity, 620 to 735 kgr.; resistance to bending, 4·53 to 6·18 kgr.

Torsion.—Oak warps considerably unless carefully seasoned. Limit of elasticity = 0·4 to 0·54 kgr.; modulus of elasticity, 612·5 to 785 kgr.; resistance to torsion, 0·75 to 0·97 kgr.

Resistance to shearing-stress, in the direction of the fibres = 0·61 to 0·97 kgr.; perpendicular to them, 1·9 to 3·49 kgr.

(7) *Resistance to Splitting.*—Oak is easily split into tolerably smooth and even staves, and is much employed for this purpose.

(8) *Hardness.*—Oak is neither the hardest and heaviest, nor the most supple and toughest of woods, but it combines in a useful manner the average of these qualities. Good oak is hard, firm, and compact, and with a glossy surface, and varies much; young oak is often tougher, more cross-grained, and harder to work than older wood. According to Gayer, if we call the resistance which the beech offers to the saw, applied

transverse to the fibres, 1, then that of freshly-felled oak = 1·09.

(9) *Durability.*—A mild climate and open situation produces the most durable oak, and it is extraordinarily durable under water, in the earth, or exposed to wind and weather, or under shelter; in the latter case it becomes more and more brittle as years roll by.

The alburnum becomes rotten usually in a few years if exposed, and is the prey of insects if under cover. The heart, if sound, may last for centuries under cover and well ventilated, and even in earth or water will endure for several generations. There are, for instance, in the museum at Kew, a portion of a pile from old London Bridge which was taken up in 1827 after having been in use for about 650 years, and a piece of a beam from the Tower of London of which it is stated that it was 'probably coeval with the building of the Tower by William Rufus;' and many other specimens of very old oak are known.

(10) *Burning Properties.*—The calorific power of oak wood is high, in accordance with its density, but it splutters and crackles and blackens too much. Nevertheless, it produces a valuable charcoal. Hartig says that if we call the cooking-power of a given volume of beech 1, that of an equal volume of oak =0·92 to 0·96.

(11) *Peculiarities.*—Oak timber is apt to suffer from various diseases, and from frost-cracks and star-shakes, cup-shakes, &c., as we shall see in the next chapter. It often presents brittle wood, red-rot (foxiness), white-rot,

spottiness of various kinds, and is sometimes twisted.
At the roots it is very often affected with burrs. It contains gallic acid, and so corrodes iron nails, clamps, &c.

(12) *Uses.*—Owing to its high price and great specific
weight oak has suffered in competition with spruce,
larch, and pine so far as building is concerned; but its
uses are very various and widespread, nevertheless, and
it is invaluable to the engineer and builder wherever
strength and durability are aimed at.

As already said, its great value depends on its
marvellous combinations of several average properties;
and considerable variations in the density, durability,
ease of working, and beauty when worked, and so forth,
are met with according to the situation and climate in
which the oak grows. Generally speaking, it is found
that when the oak grows isolated in plains, in rich soil
and a mild climate (habitat of *Q. pedunculata*), it
grows rapidly, and produces a wood of very tough and
horny consistency, which is regarded as the best for
naval and hydraulic work, cartwrights, &c., and wherever strength, tenacity, and solidity are required in
high degree (fig. 39, top). The best should have broad
and equal rings, but not broader than 7 to 8 mm., with
narrow vascular zone and the smallest possible vessels,
and with a pale, rather than dark, and even colour on
the fresh section. It should also have long fibres and
a strong, fresh smell.

In close, high forest, on poor soil, and in a rougher
climate, it may take 300 years to reach 0·6 metre diameter,

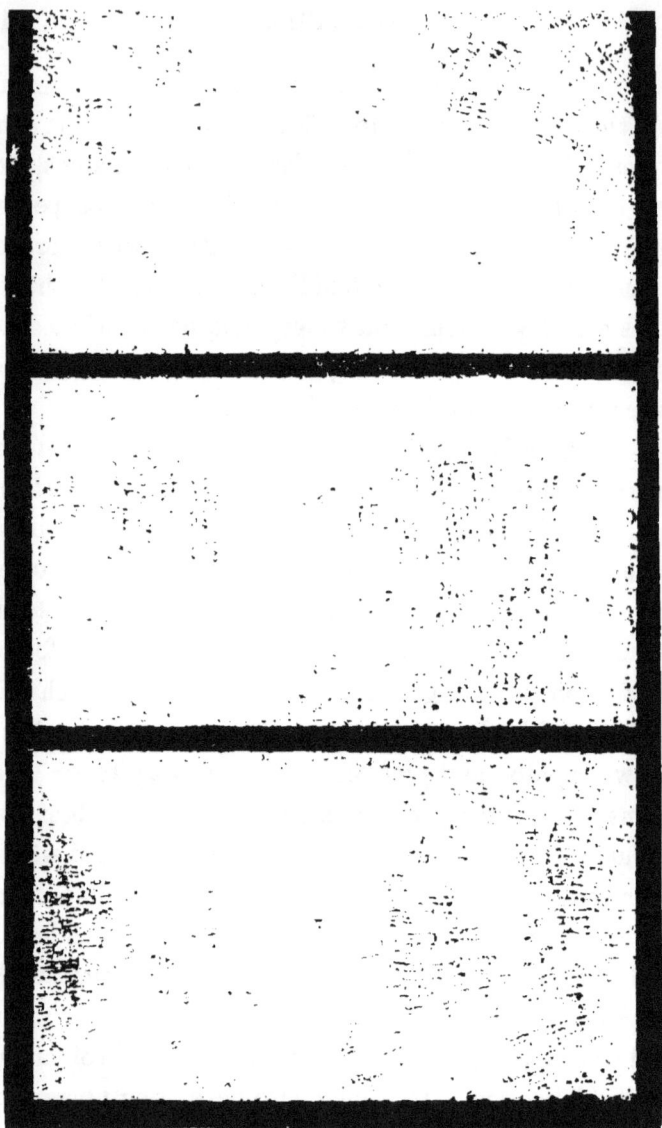

FIG. 39.—Three specimens of oak grown under different conditions.

The upper one is from a rapidly-grown tree, in the open, and at a low altitude ; the wood is very strong, hard, and heavy (density 0·827), because there is a preponderance of fibres in the broad rings. The middle specimen comes from a tree growing slowly in a forest at a considerable altitude ; the narrow rings have too large a proportion of vessels, whence the wood is soft (density 0·691), porous, and weak. The lower section is from a tree which has grown very irregularly on poor soil, as shown by the variable rings ; only the parts with broad rings are good— hence bad wood predominates (density 0·712). (Nanquette-Boppe.)

and the wood is then softer and more porous, beautifully speckled, and shrinking little (fig. 39, middle). Such wood is excellent for sculpture and carving, and is very pretty; it is also well adapted for cooperage.

In deep soil of moderate quality, in hilly country, and growing as coppice under standards, we have a wood of irregular growth and not very valuable, but useful in an all-round way for sawing and splitting (fig. 39, bottom).

Speaking generally, it is found that, other things being equal, the most resistant, closest, and toughest timber comes from isolated trees growing in the open; straight and long timber, less marked for the above qualities, comes, on the contrary, from trees grown in close, high forest. This is the conclusion arrived at by the naval authorities in France and England, and may be accepted as according with the facts of structure, &c. Some differences may be put down to the varieties, but probably Boppe is right in concluding that rate of growth, &c. due to differences in the soil and climate are the determining causes.

The builder employs oak for sills, staircase treads, keys, wedges and trenails, gate-posts and doors, and superior joinery.

Railway-sleepers are best made of young oak, as it is denser, and the Austrians say such sleepers last from seven to ten years if not treated, and for as long as sixteen years if treated with zinc chloride and other preservatives.

L

On the Continent heavy oak is used in machines, for axletrees, spokes, stamps of mills, anvil-stocks, hammer handles, &c.

Oak is much used for carving of all kinds, large furniture, panelling, parquetry, for the felloes, spokes, and axles of wheels, and for other parts of waggons, &c. In cooperage it is much used for the staves, &c., of casks, measures, sieves.

Split oak makes excellent palings and shingles, and oak vine-props are only second to those of *chestnut.* Walking-sticks are also made of oak, and even water-pipes have been used, but they taint the water.

CHAPTER XI

THE CULTIVATION OF THE OAK, AND THE DISEASES AND INJURIES TO WHICH IT IS SUBJECT

THE oak has been cultivated in all kinds of ways, but by far the best timber is produced in what is called 'high forest'—that is, the young trees all start at the same age and planted much closer together than they will be later on, their number being lessened period after period by successive removals until there is left a forest of large trees at equal distances. As it takes from 140 to 200 years to bring such a crop of timber to maturity, we may easily understand that such are rarely met with except as State forests, and the governments of various countries keep them going at various ages : one set of plantations will be ten, another twenty, a third thirty years old, for instance, when a given set is ready to be finally cut over for heavy timber.

There are many difficulties, however, in cultivating pure oak woods, and the custom of mixing other trees is a common one, for the young oaks need much light ; and yet, if each plant has the space given it necessary to allow of this light, it grows into a short and spreading

tree instead of rising up into a tall, straight one.   The
forester usually gets over these difficulties by planting
beech, or silver fir or some other species among the
oaks, but in such a way that the oaks are never completely shaded by the other trees—that is to say, he
keeps the trees at different ages, the beech, hornbeam,
silver fir, spruce, &c., only being allowed to just close
in the forest, leaving the leaf-crowns of the oaks to
be fully exposed to the light above.   The oak grows
faster than the beech or spruce, for instance, while
young, and so keeps its head easily above the others
for a time.   Very often the oak is cultivated pure at
first, and then, when the oaks are becoming too crowded
and he has to thin them, the forester puts in the
silver fir or beech, which prevents the light coming
in to the lower parts of the young oak-trees, and consequently prevents the development of lower branches,
which would give the spreading, squat habit he wishes
to prevent.   For without light the leaves of the
lower twigs of course cannot make the materials to
strengthen and thicken the latter into branches, and
so they die off, and the trunk remains a straight, clean
cylinder.

Although oaks are often raised from seed, a number
of veteran trees being allowed to stand for many years
in order to scatter the acorns, yet in by far the greater
number of cases the plants are put in artificially, the
long tap-roots being first cut in order to make them
throw out lateral rootlets.   It is also a common practice

to cut back oaks, and allow them to sprout into what is known as coppice—that is to say, numerous buds which would not have developed at all are impelled to grow up into twigs and branches (stool-shoots) from the lower parts of the cut tree. It was very usual at one time to grow oak in this way for the sake of the bark, which was employed in tanning, the trees being cut back again and again, and renewing the coppice growth after each cutting.

There are various other modes of growing oak in forests, but, whatever the system employed, the following facts have to be borne in mind and provided for. The oak is a tree that requires a soil of great depth, and sufficiently open to allow of the free penetration of air and water to the subsoil; consequently many soils, otherwise rich enough, are unsuited for the culture of this tree. Again, young seedlings and plants are apt to suffer from frost unless they are protected by suitable mixtures of other plants; but such mixtures must be chosen properly, for this tree demands light and space to a degree greater than most other European trees except the larch, birch, and one or two others, and rapidly suffers if shaded or unduly crowded. Further, as compared with other European trees the oak is a tree of the plains, and requires a relatively high temperature. These requirements also accord with its adaptation to deep, rich, well-drained soil, and, taking it all round, we have to regard the oak as a tree which makes considerable demands on the locality (soil and climate) where

it grows. In return for this, however, it yields the
best of all temperate timbers.

As we have seen, the forester has to exercise considerable forethought—the outcome of long experience
—in growing oak so as to obtain long, clean stems. The
natural habit of the tree is to form a short, thick bole
and a widely spreading crown, the main branches of
which come off not far from the ground. To compel
the stem to elongate into a long pole he has to plant
other trees with it (as we have seen, beech, spruce, &c.),
which, while they keep the light off the lower parts of
the oaks, do not overtop them. This makes the trees
long and spindly at first, as they run up their leaf-
crowns higher and higher, and it is part of the forester's
art to select the exact time when he may cut away some
of the nurse trees and let in just enough, and not too
much, light and air, so that the crowns of the oaks shall
fill out more and thicken the stems. For it must never
be forgotten that the timber is laid on from substance
prepared in the leaves.

The natural shape, so to put it, of an oak-tree is
that of a wide-spreading, short-stemmed mushroom, and
such a shape is realised in the open; the forester com-
pels it to lengthen its stem as much as possible *before*
he lets it extend its crown. Hence he aims at length
first, and then lets the tree put on timber in the mass.
He does this, of course, by taking advantage of the tree's
peculiarities, and one of these is that it grows very
rapidly when young. It will be obvious that the skilled

forester also has to aim at getting as much timber as
possible on the ground in a given time, and in the case
of a tree like the oak his calculations have to be well
made beforehand, for the tree may have to stand for
from 120 to 200 years before it is cut. Left alone it
may live for 1,000 years, but the proportion of good
timber in trees after a certain age rapidly diminishes—
a fact that has also to be reckoned with.

It is quite different, however, when trees are required for seed purposes. The oak hardly bears fruit
at all before it is fifty to sixty years old, and seventy to
eighty years is a better age for the purpose; but, as
with other trees, to produce really good seed the oaks
must be isolated, or nearly so, so that they get the maximum of light and air. Consequently a modification of
procedure has to be made when seed-trees are required.

When the fruiting period has once been reached
the tree goes on producing acorns every year; but it is
noticed that heavy crops of good seeds only recur every
five (or perhaps three) years or so, the yield in the
intervals being inconsiderable. This is in accordance
with Hartig's discovery that in the beech, for instance,
the tree goes on storing up nitrogenous materials and
salts of phosphorus and potassium during the first
seventy or eighty years of its life, and then suddenly
yields these stores to the seeds; the drain is so exhaust-
ing that it requires three to five years to re-store sufficient of these substances for another 'seed-year.' The
season or weather is also concerned in the matter.

Of course there are very many other details to be considered in the technical cultivation of the oak, but enough has been said to give the reader a general account of the procedure, and I now pass to the subject of the dangers and diseases which threaten the tree at various periods in its development, and the timber afterwards.

The diseases and injuries to which the oak is subject are very numerous and various, although, compared with some other indigenous trees, it suffers remarkably little from the different dangers which await it at all stages in the course of its long life from the seedling to the aged tree. Some of these are referable to the exigencies of the non-living environments—the climate, soil, &c.; others are due to the attacks of living organisms, both vegetable and animal—from the weeds which smother the young seedlings by keeping the light from them, to man himself, who injures the trees in various ways. The earliest struggles of the young seedling are with the weeds, slugs, and insects of various kinds that invade the territory on which the acorn has germinated, and of course the baby plant has also to contend against any inclemencies of climate or unsuitableness of soil that it may meet with. Owing to such vicissitudes very many of the seedlings never obtain the dimensions of a plant at all, and in some seasons the mortality is enormous. Other destructive agents during these early phases of the life of the oak are cattle and deer, which not only tread down the shoots but also nibble them off, and mice, squirrels, &c., do their share of injury, as also do wood-pigeons and other birds.   In the North of Europe the young plants suffer terribly from the ravages of a fungus named *Rosellinia*, the mycelium of which sends its branches into the roots and kills them, consequently entailing the death of the plant.   The larvæ of various insects also damage the roots and bring about injuries which may prove fatal.   *Cynips corticalis* produces galls on the lower parts of the stems.

When the plant has passed into the condition of a sapling its dangers are for the most part of quite other nature, the injurious fungi especially being different. The chief diseases of the roots now arise from their spreading into unsuitable soil, the drainage of which may be incomplete, and thus bring about a sodden, acid, ill-aërated condition.   The want of oxygen and the low temperature combine to kill the root-hairs and young rootlets, and the leaves above part with their water faster than it can be supplied from below, and they turn yellow and die off, the branches dry up, and the tree dies.

Other dangers arise from the persistent overshadowing of other trees, which slowly kill the young oaks by depriving their leaves of light ; the offending trees playing the same inimical part, in fact, that grass and weeds, &c., play towards the small seedlings.   Or the roots may be too thickly set in the soil if the trees are too crowded, and each suffers from over-competition with others.

Much mischief is effected by the attacks of insects
of various kinds. The caterpillars of certain moths
(especially *Cnethocampa* and *Tortrix*), for instance, eat
off the leaves in June, and then form large masses of
mingled débris, skins, &c., as they pass into the pupa
stage in July. The denudation of the leaves brought

FIG. 40.—*Tortrix viridana*, the green oak-moth, the larvæ
of which eat off the young leaves. (Altum.)

about by such caterpillars is apt to be very exhaustive
to the trees, for although they put forth new foliage in
July and August, it must not be forgotten that these new
leaves are constructed from materials which should have
gone to the general stores in the tree, and from which
new wood, for instance, would have been developed.

Of other animals which injure oaks I may mention the various cattle, which bite off or rub the bark and buds; hares, squirrels, mice, &c., which nibble roots and buds and destroy the acorns, &c.; and a few birds; and certain beetles, which bore into the wood.

Among the pests belonging to the vegetable kingdom the following may be selected from a large number. The honeysuckle occasionally twists tightly round the young stem, and in course of time so compresses the cortex that the formative materials from the leaf-crown have to pass in a spiral course between the coils of the strangling plant, and the tightly-squeezed parts may be starved as the tree thickens, and even the death of the cambium may follow, especially if one or two of the honeysuckle coils come to lie nearly horizontally round the stem.

As a rare event the mistletoe is found on the oak. A much commoner parasite of the same family is *Loranthus europœus*, which does considerable damage to oaks in some parts of Europe. The sticky seeds are carried into the trees by thrushes. Here they germinate, and send their roots, or haustorial strands, into the cortex of a branch as far as the cambium, where they spread and feed on the contents of the young wood- and cambium-cells, causing malformations of the injured branch at the spot attacked owing to the hypertrophy of the tissues, to which abnormal quantities of food materials now flow (fig. 41); and frequently bringing about the death of the upper parts of the

branches owing to the paucity of water at those parts,
the parasite taking much of that which reaches the
injured place, and the impoverished wood allowing less
to pass than it would normally have done.

Among the fungi there are several enemies to the
oak-tree. The leaves are attacked by *Phyllactinia*, one

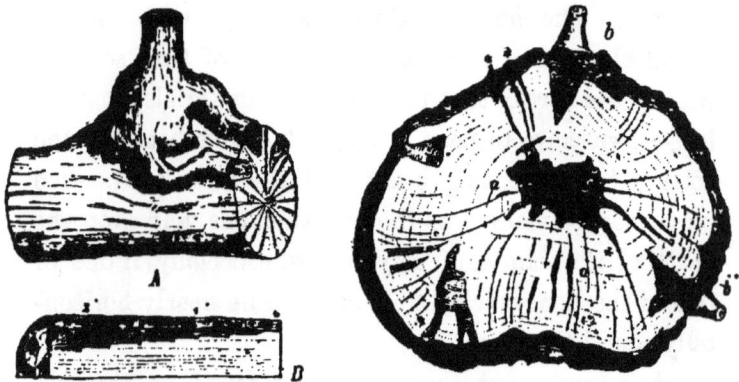

FIG. 41.—*Loranthus europæus.* A. Lower part of stem
attached to branch of oak, both denuded of cortex. B.
Longitudinal section through one of the haustorial strands,
showing its progress, year by year, as the branch thickens.
C. Transverse section, through a branch which has long
been badly infested with the *Loranthus*; *a a*, dead remains of old haustorial strands; *b b*, young *Loranthus*
plants developed as buds from the older ones. The
asterisks mark still younger specimens. (Hartig.)

of the mildews, which forms white networks, like spiders'
webs, on their surfaces. Numerous small ascomycetous
fungi are found on the dying and dead leaves, but these
do not directly injure the living tree.

Other fungi are found in the cortex, and one of the
most interesting of these is a red *Nectria*, the spores of

which germinate on the bark, but cannot infect the tree unless there is a wound in the neighbourhood. However, owing to the numerous small cracks and ruptures due to the injuries caused by insects, hail, frost, &c., the mycelium easily gains access to the cortex and cambium, and feeds on the contents of the cambium cells, which it destroys. The consequence of the irritations set up is the formation of canker-like knots on the branches, and the injury may be great enough to destroy smaller ones, and occasionally even a large one.

Unquestionably the most important of the diseases to which the older oak-trees are subject are those which result in the destruction of the timber.

There are about six or eight of the fungi known popularly as toadstools—technically as *Hymenomycetes*—which are able to injure and even destroy the timber of standing oaks, and while each of these pests does the damage in its own peculiar way, they show considerable similarity in general behaviour. In the first place, these fungi are unable to penetrate the bark of sound trees, and their hyphæ always gain access to the timber by means of actual wounds and exposed surfaces of wood, such as the cracks caused by frost or by the bending down of heavy branches under the weight of a load of snow, or the ruptured ends of broken branches blown off by strong gales or struck by falling trees, or places where animals have removed the bark, where cart-wheels have abraded the larger roots, and so on. Once inside, the hyphæ of these fungi pierce the vessels, cells, &c., of

the wood by excreting soluble ferments which dissolve
the substance of their walls, and feed on the products of
solution. Hence they damage the timber in two ways
—they riddle it through and through by myriads of
minute apertures, and thus ruin its structure, and they

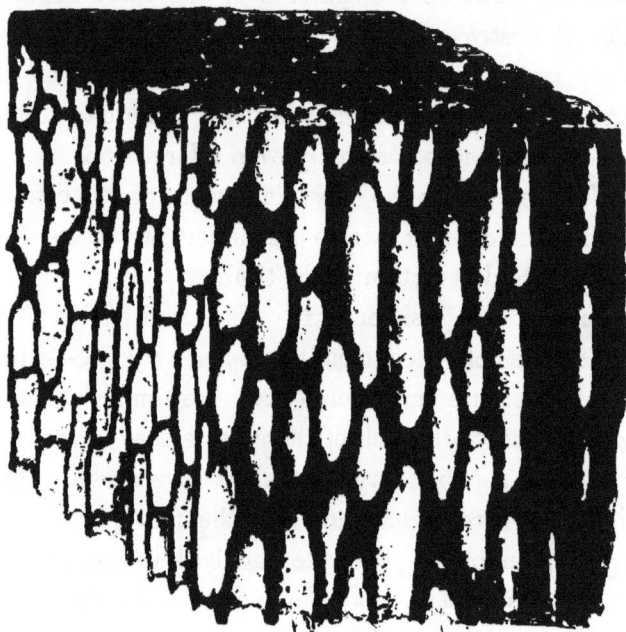

FIG. 42.—Piece of oak destroyed by *Thelephora Perdix*,
showing the characteristic markings due to the action
of the fungus. (R. Hartig.)

reduce its substance by dissolving it and converting it
to their own uses. The wood, therefore, loses in strength
and in weight, and becomes 'rotten.' There are differences in detail as to the mode of destroying the elements
of the wood, but the final result is much the same in all

cases—some of the fungi destroy the vessels, fibres, &c., by dissolving their walls from inside, while others destroy the part common to contiguous cells, &c., and thus first isolate the elements and then complete the destruction. A series of very interesting researches by

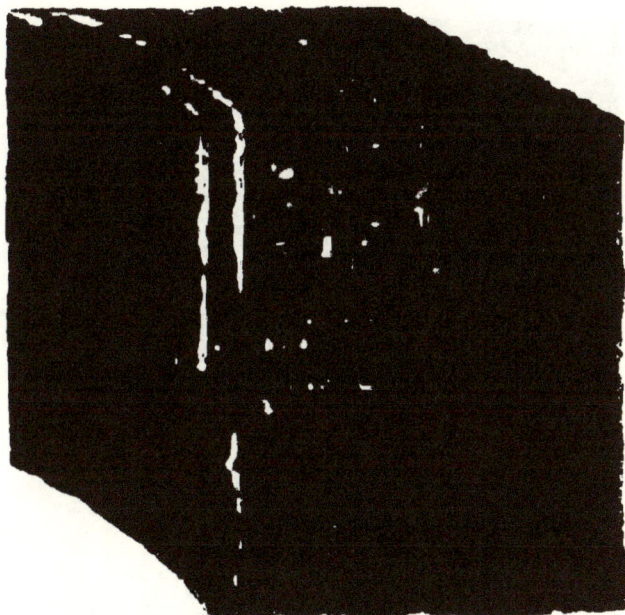

FIG. 43.—Oak timber destroyed by the fungus *Hydnum diversidens*. *a* shows the medullary rays on the tangential section; *b*, a mass of felted mycelium. (R. Hartig.)

Hartig has demonstrated that the presence of these timber-destroying fungi can be detected from the markings and discolorations they produce in the wood; those due to *Hydnum diversidens, Thelephora Perdix, Polyporus sulphureus, P. igniarius, P. dryadeus,* and *Stereum*

hirsutum being all different, and in some cases so characteristic that the merest glance suffices to diagnose the
disease (*cf.* figs. 42 to 45).

There is yet another disease of oak timber to be
noticed, and one which causes great havoc in buildings

FIG. 44.—Oak damaged by *Polyporus igniarius,* a very
common timber fungus.   (R. Hartig.)

where the ventilation is bad and the air damp.   This is
the too well known dry-rot, due to the destructive
action of the fungus *Merulius lacrymans,* a hymenomy-
cete allied to the preceding, but differing from them in
not attacking the standing timber.   The spores of this
fungus are able to infect oak planks, beams, &c.; and

the mycelium rapidly spreads on and in the wood, destroying the cell-walls, and causing the wood to shrink and crack and warp, and finally to fall to pieces. Thorough ventilation is fatal to the fungus and stops · the rot.

A series of enemies to the oak-tree not yet referred

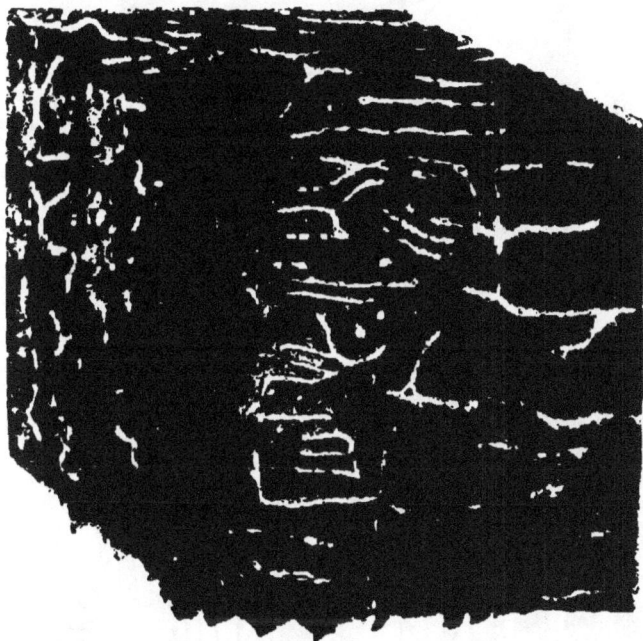

FIG. 45.—Oak wood destroyed by *Polyporus dryadeus*, showing the very characteristic markings, like insect tunnels in a deep red-brown matrix. (R. Hartig.)

to are various gall-insects, so called because they pierce the young leaves or buds, &c., and lay their eggs in the wound ; the irritation set up suffices to induce a flow of food materials to the stimulated spot, and the overfed

M

FIG. 46.—Piece of oak-bark with fructification of *Polyporus sulphureus.*

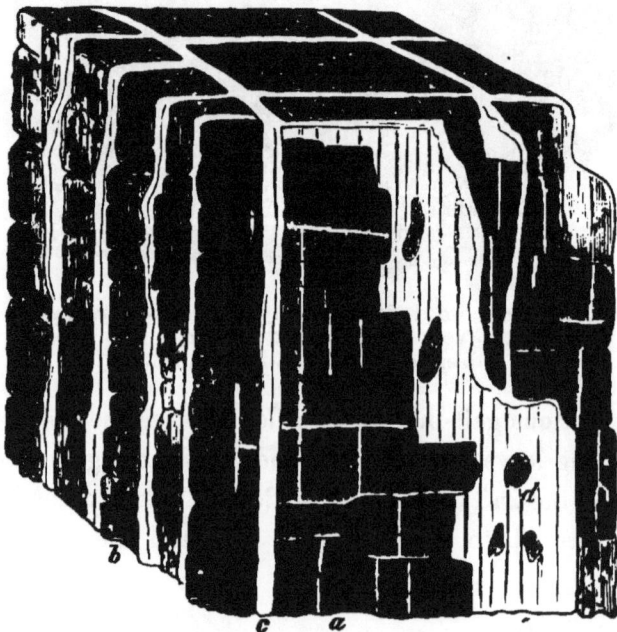

FIG. 47.—Piece of oak attacked by *Polyporus sulphureus,* the yellowish-white mycelium of which is seen at *c* and *d.*   (R. Hartig.)

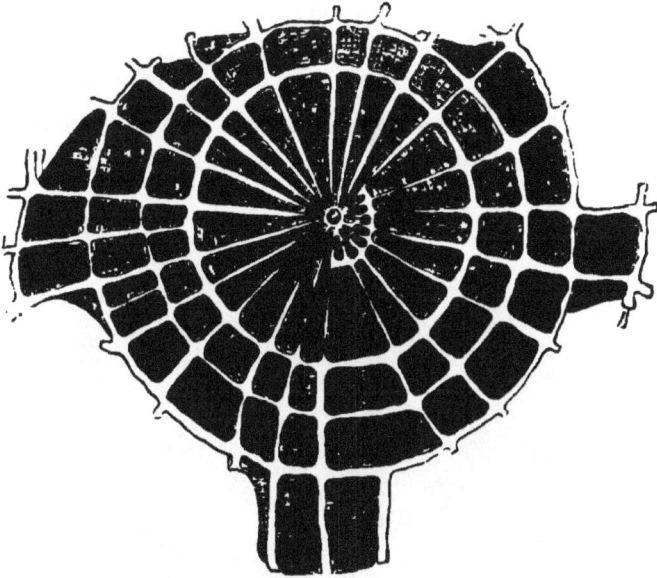

FIG. 48.—Transverse section of oak timber destroyed by
Polyporus sulphureus. (R. Hartig.)

FIG. 49.—Highly magnified longitudinal radial section of
a piece of oak destroyed by a timber fungus, showing
the ravages of the hyphæ in the various tissues. (R.
Hartig.)

cells multiply and form the gall. This is a mere outline sketch of the matter, however, for the differences in
behaviour are enormous. Each insect causes the forma-

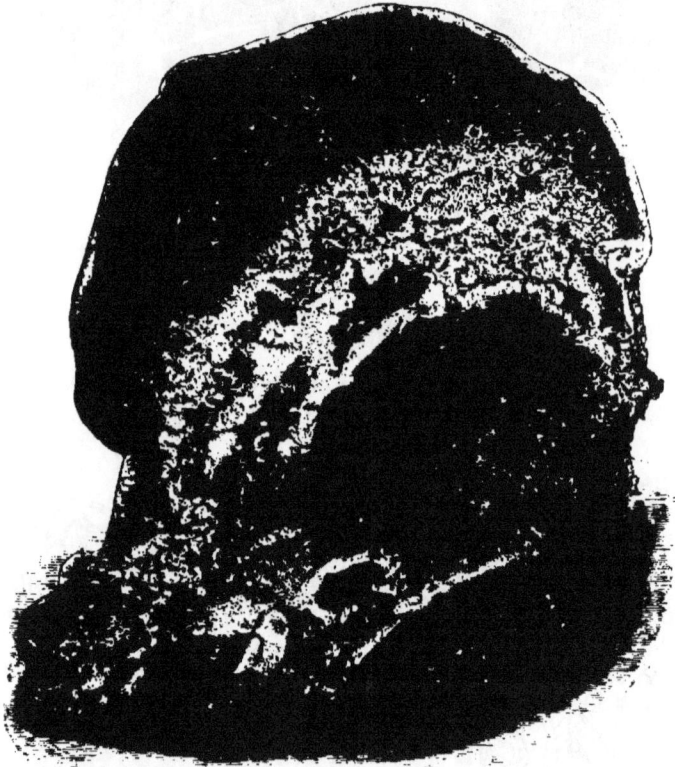

FIG. 50.—Portion of the spore-bearing hymenium of *Merulius lacrymans*, the fungus of 'dry rot.'

tion of a specific kind of gall, differing in shape, size,
colour, and other characters from those caused by other
gall-insects. There are many kinds, and only a few can
be mentioned here. Each species of oak may have its

own galls also, those on the American oaks differing
from those on the European species, but some are common

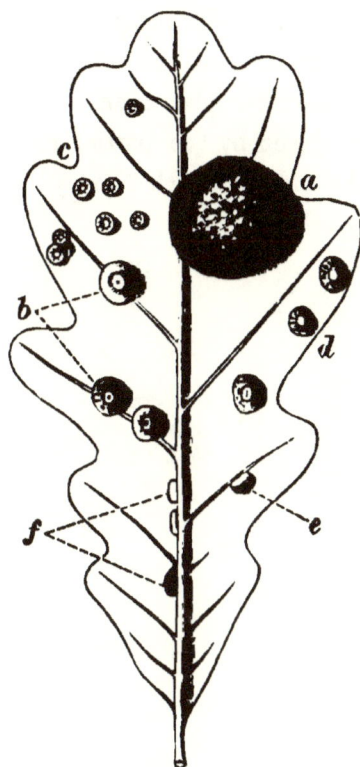

FIG. 51.—An oak-leaf with several kinds of Cynips galls
on it. *a*, gall produced by *Cynips scutellaris*; *b*, *C. divisa*;
c, *Neuroterus Reaumurii*; *e*, *Biorhiza renum*; *f*, *Neuroterus ostreus*. (Frank.)

to more than one species. The insects which produce
the commonest English oak-galls are nearly all members
of the *Cynipideœ*, a group of hymenoptera which lay

their eggs in the young tissues of various plants, especially oaks and roses.

Some of the resulting galls are discoid, such as the 'oak-spangles' of our woods; others, again, are spherical, such as the common leaf-galls so well known in England, and the so-called oak-apple; then there are the 'artichoke galls,' produced by the partial metamorphosis of the buds of the oak in which the cynips has laid its egg, and many others.

CHAPTER XII

RELATIONSHIPS OF THE OAKS—THEIR DISTRIBUTION
IN SPACE AND TIME

THE oak is a member of a very large and ancient group
of dicotyledonous flowering plants, embracing the
beeches, chestnuts, hazel-nuts, &c., and many other
forest trees of the Northern Hemisphere.

The number of species of oaks (*Quercus*) is very
large, probably more than 300, of which the majority
belong to North America, Europe, China, Japan, and
other parts of Asia. There are none in Africa south of
the Mediterranean region, nor in South America or
Australasia. Some remarkable species are found in the
Himalayas, and many in the Malayan Archipelago.

The various species of the genus *Quercus* are
arranged into groups according to differences in the
form and arrangement of the scales of the cupule, the
characters of the leaves, and certain peculiarities in the
acorns. Many oaks, especially those of warm countries,
for instance, are 'evergreen,' with hard, leathery leaves,
quite unlike the leaves of our common British oak.

The latter is denominated botanically as *Quercus Robur*, but certain varietal forms of it have been distinguished, of which the commonest in this country are *Q. pedunculata*, a variety with the female flowers on long peduncles, and *Q. sessiliflora*, with the female flowers on short peduncles; but although numerous attempts have been made to define these forms, and while small differences in the petioles, lobing of the leaves, and the wood, &c., have been insisted upon at various times by observers, it appears that the two varieties graduate into one another by intermediate forms. In England the variety *pedunculata* is the commonest over the country generally, but in the hilly districts of North Wales and the North of England the variety *sessiliflora* is said to prevail. Similarly, on the Continent the latter variety is found at higher elevations than the former, though its area of occurrence is more restricted. This pronounced variability of the oak was commented upon by the late Charles Darwin, who points out in the 'Origin of Species,' that more than a dozen species have been made by a certain author out of what other botanists regard as mere varieties of the common oak.

De Candolle, who made a special study of this group, found the variations so enormous that, although he made something like 300 species, he concluded that the majority of these were merely provisional; and he concluded, as others have done, that we have in the numerous varieties of the species this old genus *Quercus*, series of incipient species. If the connecting forms were to die out, leaving certain varieties more isolated than they are at present, systematists would elevate the latter to the rank of species.

It is interesting to observe that twenty-eight varieties of the common English oak (*Q. Robur*) have been described, and that the majority of these can be grouped around the three forms *pedunculata, sessiliflora,* and *pubescens*, the latter being a somewhat hairy variety found on the Continent. No doubt we have here, again, a case where the three varieties mentioned would be accorded specific rank if the connecting forms died out, as some of them appear to be doing.

I have already stated that the oaks are a very ancient family, and their great variability is in accordance with this. It probably implies that the genus has had time during its migrations over the Northern Hemisphere to vary immensely, and that some of the varieties have become adapted to given situations, others to others. On the whole, the oak family must be regarded as a northern type which has sent extensions southward.

Now let us glance at their geological history. Something like 200 forms of fossil oaks have been described from remains, chiefly of leaves and wood, found in various parts of the world. Some of the European fossil forms remind us of species now found only in hot countries near the tropics, others are peculiar, and some are very doubtful.

The earliest remains of oaks come from the Creta-

ceous strata, being coeval with the first undoubted dico-
tyledons that have been found. Many have been found
in the Tertiary also, and we have to conclude that the
oaks were probably already a well-developed group of
plants before the higher mammalia existed—*i.e.* so far
as we can judge from the fragmentary records of the
rocks. It seems that even the present species of oaks
were already in existence in Tertiary times, and possibly
some of their varieties also.

From the evidence of their fossil remains, together
with the facts of their present distribution, it is at least
exceedingly probable that the European oaks, including
our English oak, came into existence somewhere in the
East, and that, after spreading from Asia towards the
West, they are now slowly retreating before competing
forms—*e.g.* the beech. Meanwhile the English oak
(*Q. Robur*) has been giving rise to several varieties, of
which three at least (viz. *pedunculata, sessiliflora,* and
pubescens) have become sufficiently marked to be regarded as species by those who do not consider the connecting forms.

It is not improbable that this migration of the
European oaks from Asia was completed before the
islands of Sicily, Sardinia, Corsica, and Britain were
separated from the mainland of the Continent. Moreover, our English oak is not distantly related to certain
species of Eastern Asia and of Western North America,
and it has been surmised that all these related forms
sprang from a common ancestor not unlike our English

oak of to-day. Again, fossil leaves from Italy, found in diluvial deposits, are so like those of certain Californian oaks now existing that a common origin is also suggested, and similar leaves have been discovered in Tertiary deposits in North-west America. If all the evidence is put together we may conclude with Asa Gray that ' the probable genealogy of *Q. Robur*, traceable in Europe up to the commencement of the present epoch, looks eastward and far into the past on far distant shores.'

Many of the oaks yield products which are made use of in the arts, apart from their timber, the most valuable of which comes from our European oak, the white oaks of North America, and one or two Himalayan species. In several countries oaks are grown for the sake of the bark, cups, &c., as a tanning material, and these even form important articles of export. Quercitron, a yellow dye and tanning material, is obtained from *Q. tinctoria* in North America.

Cork, as used for bottling and other purposes, is obtained in Spain, the South of France, and in Algiers, from the thick periderm of *Q. Suber*.

Q. infectoria yields the chief galls of commerce. They are caused by the punctures of *Cynips gallæ tinctoriæ*, and are used for making ink and for dyeing. In these and similar galls the value depends on the presence of relatively large quantities of tannic and gallic acids which they contain.

INDEX

www.ingramcontent.com/pod-product-compliance
Lightning Source LLC
Chambersburg PA
CBHW030846270326
41928CB00007B/1236